SECOND PLACE IS THE FIRST WINNER

SECOND PLACE IS THE FIRST WINNER

A MEMOIR OF REJECTION AND RESILIENCE

ROBERT HARRIS III

Second Place is the First Winner
A Memoir of Rejection and Resilience
by Robert Harris III
Copyright © 2020

Paperback ISBN: 978-1-952561-04-7
eBook ISBN: 978-1-952561-05-4

Edited by Folusho Ayeni
Get It Done Publishing
4410 Stacks Road Atlanta, GA 30349
www.getitdonepublishing.com

Ashley King, Publisher
Get It Done Publishing eBook Edition 2020
Get It Done Publishing Paperback Edition 2020

Printed in the USA

Join our Get It Done Publishing Readers Group for sneak previews, updates, new projects, and giveaways. Sign up at getitdonepublishing.com.

I want to thank all of the women that have positively influenced my life and made me the man I am today.

My fiancée Raven, my daughter Robin, my Grandma America, Grandma Lib, and Grandma Odessa Jones, my other moms Ms. Jackie Shipley and Lettie Robinson, my sister Anissa Shipley, my foster mom Mrs. Bethel, my teacher Mrs. Barrett, Ms. Sharon, Mrs. Connie Wilson, my principal Mrs. Allen. Last but not least, my angel in heaven, my momma Donna Harris.

"Respect the Queens, never treat them badly or foul, too y'all I actually bow. God said any of us can carry a gun, but only made the woman strong enough to carry a child" - Chess

CONTENTS

RESILIENT

From the age of seven up to college, my life was lived in and out of the foster care system. For much of that time, even as a kid, I felt like many of the homes I was in were only in it for the money. But my life didn't start there. In fact, before foster care, life was actually pretty good.

Now to start off, my mom's name was Donna, and she had eight kids altogether: Tymane, me, Dontoya, Quadarrell, Anthony, Sheronda, Latoya, and another son named Anthony. When she was just sixteen she had my older brother Tymane, but we all called him Camp. I came along next, a few years later, and then somewhere around when I was three, she had had my little sister Dontoya by a man named Herman.

The earliest I can remember, though, is me, Camp, and Dontoya living with Dontoya's dad, Herman. The short time our mom was with him, life was good for all of us. Herman and my mom's relationship was pretty solid, and even though he wasn't me and my brother's biological dad, he didn't take care of us any differently from our younger sister.

Herman had a big family and they all really took us on as their own. His mom was my Grandma Lib, and she was like the family matriarch. I loved that lady. Granddaddy Hunch was a cool man, and he was the one who taught me how to cook. That's where my love for cooking started.

We all lived in the projects of Cotter Homes in Louisville, Kentucky, but we never lacked for anything. Really, we lived something like a glamorous lifestyle which wouldn't have made sense to anybody on the outside looking in, but Herman was such a successful drug dealer, he just had it like that.

He was always buying us a bunch of toys, even though we had so many. Kids would try to spend the night with us, just so they could steal our toys! It was nothing for him to have different people coming in to do different household chores, and I didn't realize until later that they were actually maids. Rolls Royces were common, and our place was a revolving door for different types of celebrities, music artists, and actors...Muhammad Ali even showed up at one point!

Once, me and Herman were sitting outside, and I was upset because Camp had a bike and had rolled off without me. I was crying hard and looking at some other dudes in the neighborhood riding around on their bikes, when Herman said to me, "You want that bike?"

I thought he was going to go get me one, so I said, "Yeah!"

Instead he called the guy over, said something to him, and just like that...I had a bike!

That night, Camp came home but this time I had a BMX bike. It was his turn to be jealous. I didn't even know how to ride a bike, but I had one though!

Like I said, life was pretty good. Herman also had a big family, and there was always a gathering or party going on. Even if our mom or Herman wasn't around, we knew there were other people in the neighborhood that we could go to. For the time they were together, I knew what it was like to have some type of stability, and we didn't lack for anything.

I didn't really know it then, but Herman was what some would call 'hood rich,' and he kept his 'business' in order. I remember he kept certain things in the room he and my mom shared. In fact, that is part of what I believe led to my mom getting on drugs and where things changed for the worse.

One particular day my mom was driving with my little sister, and they got into a really bad car accident. Dontoya got glass all in her face, and my mom broke her arm badly. I don't know for sure how things happened, but I think she needed to ease her pain somehow. It seems natural to me that since we were already living with Herman, she started sneaking drugs from his stash.

I don't know how long it was before he started noticing, or if he always knew and was waiting for her to come clean or what, but I do know this was the beginning of a long downward spiral for my mom, Camp, and me.

Things also started getting tense on Herman's end with his family, and they began to experience a lot of trouble. One morning, Camp and I were walking out the door to go to school when suddenly Camp started yelling like he had lost his mind. I looked where he was staring and didn't really understand what I was seeing, but I started screaming too. My mom opened the door back up, glanced outside, and pulled us back in, all while calling for Herman.

Someone had kidnapped Herman's youngest brother, our uncle Glen, who was nineteen and sliced his body over one hundred times, bled him to death, and then propped his body upon a tree outside of our building.

I didn't completely realize what I saw until I got older, but after we went to his funeral, Herman set out on a mission to find revenge. One of the first times we ever saw Herman with a gun was when Camp and I were sitting in our mom's room watching TV. He came into the room, went to the closet, and came back out with a gun. We both jumped back, and when he noticed how scared we were, he stopped and explained how much he loved us and how he would never hurt us. But he still left with the gun.

He started going on killing sprees, and it really took a straining toll on their family, especially Herman. He was the oldest, so I can only imagine the type of responsibility and guilt he felt.

So with all these different situations going on, Herman

just started backing off of my mom. We could tell he was putting space between them, especially when he just stopped living with us and started messing with this other lady named Princess while we were still living in Cotter Homes. He took my little sister Dontoya with him; I guess because he saw what direction my mom was going in. He would still come by to see us, but he just wouldn't stay there or spend the night. Mom would get into fights with Princess, and things weren't getting any better because she continued to use drugs.

Since I was so young, I'm not too sure exactly when my mom got pregnant again, but somewhere around this time is when my mom had Quadarrell. Because she was on drugs, he died only a few days after she gave birth. Looking back at it now, I know this probably took a toll on her even more than I could see.

During Christmas that year, when Herman and my mom were backing off from each other, we had almost fifty presents under the tree that had been steadily building up. Christmas Eve we went to bed, and the next day, when we woke up, the gifts were completely gone. My mom had taken everything and sold them, all just to get money to buy more drugs. Nothing like that had ever happened before, and it shocked me so much as a kid who was used to always having presents. That's when I knew something was definitely wrong.

My birthday is in February, and even though we had had that crazy Christmas, I was still expecting something. But the only thing I got was, "Hey, it's your birthday!"

Then April came around, and I remember being so jealous of Camp because my mom got him a bag of penny candy. It might not have been so bad if I had even just gotten one thing: a candy bar, a dollar, or something! I wanted his candy so bad, but that's just how bad things were getting.

Right around here is when my mom met Kim. Kim seemed to be a pretty decent guy at first, probably because he started hanging around our apartment instead of moving in with us. Basically, he seemed like someone to get my mom's mind off of Herman, now that he had kind of moved on. He was nice enough to my brother and me, and eventually, my mom told Camp and me, "Hey, we're moving."

We moved from Cotter Homes to the West End of Louisville, where he convinced my mom to buy a house that needed some work done on it. It was a two-story shotgun house, and it literally had no kitchen and almost no flooring. You could look down, through the floor, and be staring at the foundation. There was no stove, no refrigerator, none of the things you really needed for a house to be functional...but I guess they were just caught up in the idea of having one. It wasn't too bad of an idea, but the problem was they never really got around to finishing it. The worst thing about this move though, was that Kim flipped on us like a light switch.

Kim had never been mean to us before. But as soon as we moved into that house, he started treating us like we were some random bums from the street. He started calling Camp and me all types of names and cussing us out. He didn't put his hands on us, but it was also the beginning of watching months of mental and physical abuse towards my mom.

Stuff like this became normal, and my mom would leave the house for days at a time to escape. Since we weren't Kim's kids and he didn't have my mom there to abuse, he would get up and go, too.

"She ain't gon' keep leaving me with y'all. Fuck y'all, I' ma leave too!"

So Camp and I ended up being those kids who would knock on doors asking for food because there would be literally nothing in the house to eat. We would bum for baloney and hot dogs from neighbors. People don't believe me when I tell them, but we learned how to make rice by putting an iron upside down in a shoebox and cooking on it. There was nowhere we could go and no one to play with, so we would do stuff like wrapping ourselves up in sheets and throw ourselves down the stairs.

One day we were having a barbeque at home, and one of Kim's friends came over. Mom was cooking and asked us if we wanted hot dogs, but when Kim responded to her, they started having a heated conversation, back and forth. The next thing we knew, Kim just walked over and punched my mom right in the nose, as simple as if he were walking over to get a hot dog. Me and my brother could only stare in shock as blood started gushing out of our mom's nose. We tried to run over to her, but Kim's friend seemed to appear right behind us and grabbed us back to keep us still. Mom was bent over the sink, trying so hard to wave at us to calm down, stop the flow of blood, and reassure us at the same time, "I'm OK, baby, i—it's OK."

The situation with Kim took one last turn for the worse. I was outside playing in the yard one day when I saw my mom come running out of the house with Kim chasing after her. He grabbed her, pulling them down to the ground, and they started tumbling over each other, kicking and hitting each other the whole time. Normally I stayed out of it, but this time I couldn't contain myself; I was tired of watching my mom get beat up. I grabbed a stick, ran over to them, and started hitting Kim with it, yelling and screaming for him to get off of my mom. It didn't seem like I was too effective, but somehow, I managed to poke him right in the eye. He fell back off of her, clutching his eye and screaming. He looked and me, and I looked at him, and I had a split second of realization before I took off running.

I could hear Kim chasing after me, hollering for me too, "Get back here!" One part of me was relieved he wasn't hitting my mom anymore, but I knew if he caught me, it wouldn't turn out good for me at all.

He was going to kill me!

Running as fast as I could and breathing as hard as my lungs would let me, I rounded a corner and saw one of the older neighborhood boys standing in his yard. I had always looked up to him, and at that moment, the only thing I could think to do was to run to him.

I ran up to him, wrapped my arms around his legs, and said, "Help me, help me, he's gonna kill me!" Kim finally caught up with me and was right outside of his yard about to run in after me, but the boy said to him in so many words, "So you're really gonna fight a little kid? Come on my property if you want, watch what happens!" They stood face to face, staring each other down, and I was only halfway sure Kim would back down. When he actually did, I was amazed! Here was this boy who was only a few years older than me, but he was able to make Kim back off with only a few strong threats! He literally became my hero for that moment.

Still, even though I was saved from Kim's wrath, he kicked us out of the house that night, and we ended up spending the night sleeping on picnic tables in a park. The next day, we went to stay with my aunt Cora and uncle Joe. The only good thing that really came out of this situation with Kim is Sheronda. Again, I don't know for sure, since as a young boy I wasn't keeping tabs on my mom, but around this time is when she got pregnant again. The real giveaway that makes me think Kim was the father is because they both had the same light-colored, pretty eyes. But Sheronda was eventually put in another foster home when she was younger, and I wouldn't get to meet her until we were both a lot older.

We were at Aunt Cora and Uncle Joe's for a few days together, but my mom's habit picked back up by that time, and she left me and my brother by ourselves again at their house. We must have been there too many days without our mom saying anything to them, because my aunt called

Child Protective Services, and we were taken away from our mom for the first time.

My brother and I were temporarily placed in a group foster home called the Home of The Innocents, before we were put in our first foster home with a woman named Ms. Robie. As our first foster mom, she was about as indifferent as could be. She wasn't especially mean, but she really didn't do much for us beyond the basics. We took showers, but they were cold. We stayed downstairs in the basement where there were concrete floors, but they didn't help much when it came to keeping heat. Ms. Robie put a kerosene heater down there with us, but the heater was so small that you had to put your body almost right on top of it to really feel any warmth.

I was so desperately cold one day that I found myself drawing closer and closer to it to try to warm myself up, and I ended up getting burned on my leg. The whole house was just physically cold, but it really seemed just like an extension of Ms. Robie's attitude towards us: cold and indifferent. She didn't go out of her way to antagonize us or anything, but she didn't go the extra mile for us either. This was the first time when I truly felt like someone was only 'taking care' of us for the money.

Things went from bad to worse in foster care when they took us out of Ms. Robie's home and put us with a woman named Ms. Jackson. Unlike Ms. Robie's cold and distant attitude, Ms. Jackson's demeanor was very mean, and she seemed to be intentional about it. Whenever we would talk about our life with Herman and how we used to live, she made sure to tell us we were lying, saying things to us like, "Y'all didn't have no maids helping you" or call us, "triflin' ass little niggas." I was too young to realize why at the time, but it seemed like just us talking about how we used to live a nice life made her even more determined to be spiteful towards us. Even though she lived in a rather nice neighborhood, it wasn't to actually provide a good home for us or for any of the other kids; it was literally to prove she had a 'good' living environment so she could continue to get money for fostering kids.

She would make us eat oatmeal with nothing to sweeten it except peppermints, even though she was getting more than enough money to help take care of us. We would sit there for almost an hour, watching the clock tick by, waiting for a peppermint to slowly melt from oatmeal that was losing heat the longer we waited. By the time it finally melted, the oatmeal would be cold, but we'd still be forced to eat it. It was disgusting.

The first time I ever passed out was at her house, and it just made no sense. Here was a home that looked fine on the outside and was in a great neighborhood, and here was a woman who kept up such a façade that she was able to foster children continuously...but we were starving and miserable.

My mom finally came back around from being in and out of the streets, and at this point, my life was starting to feel like a constant revolving door. Whether it was my mom coming in and going out for days or weeks at a time, or me and my brother bouncing back and forth to different places and foster homes, I didn't have too much real stability during this period in life. My mom would meet different people, and who they were usually had a direct impact on whether we were stable or not.

Mom had got a little piece of an apartment right off of Oak Street, overlooking Shelby Park. It was so small; it must have been a studio because I don't remember there being a bedroom in it at all. This was when she had our little brother, Anthony.

Money was so tight; my mom couldn't afford diapers, so she had these white cloth diapers for Anthony. She would have me and my brother take turns washing them, and I remember being so addicted to washing his diapers and getting them back completely white, that I would even take Camp's turn to make sure the diapers were cleaned all the way. To this day, I have a love for laundry, and I'm big on white home goods!

Eventually, mom lost the apartment from not paying rent, but across the street and maybe three houses down was a woman she had met named Ms. Sharon. I didn't know her that well at first, but I think my mom got to know her because she would do drugs with one of Ms. Sharon's sons. We were all looking at the TV one night when they started showing footage of a high-speed police chase on the news, and we realized it was our mom and Ms. Sharon's son we were seeing! They ended up getting locked up, but Ms. Sharon just kind of took us in.

She was one of the nicest people I remember meeting when I was a kid, and she immediately took a liking to me.

Even though she already had a lot of other people living with her and her kids, she let me and Camp stay there too, and I just remember her always taking me with her to different places whenever she could.

Ms. Sharon was white, and there was a lot of racial tension in that neighborhood at the time. This tension extended to the different people she had living in the house too, so I often overheard comments from other white boarders questioning why she was letting us stay there, and how she should just kick us out. But Ms. Sharon was genuinely a good woman and really cared for us like we were her own, and the other roomers knew they could only say so much before they would cross the line and potentially be kicked out themselves. So even though the tension was thick, we knew we really had nothing to worry about.

One of the big things to do in the neighborhood was to go to the Shelby Park pool. Camp, Ms. Sharon's kids, and I would go there just about every day, and this is where I learned how to swim. We would try to get there early because if you got there and helped clean it in the morning, they would let you in for free!

The bad part about the pool was that kids would steal your food while you were swimming. Ms. Sharon got tired of us complaining all the time and coming home still hungry because she would send us off with sandwiches and everything. How she did all of this, I have no idea, because she was just a waitress at Shoney's. She would work a lot, and I remember seeing her in uniform all the time, but I know money was probably short on her end too. But still, somehow, she ended up buying one of those above-ground pools and putting it in her backyard just for us so we wouldn't have to deal with the stupidity at the Shelby Park pool anymore!

By this time, my mom had got out of jail, but we were still staying with Ms. Sharon. She had met a guy in the neighborhood named Jerry. Now, before I even saw him, Camp told me he looked just like the guy Jheri Curl from *Hollywood Shuffle*...but when I *did* finally meet him, to me he looked just like the guy singing "I believe the children are the future..." from *Coming to America!*

We figured out mom and Jerry were dating, but she still told us to stay with Ms. Sharon for a while until eventually, Jerry agreed to let us move in. Jerry had two daughters, Nalona and Shaneka, so now it was me, Anthony, Camp, my mom, Jerry, and his two daughters all living together under the same roof. He happened to live just around the corner from Ms. Sharon's house, so it wasn't too far of a distance to move, and things seemed to be pretty alright with him.

One of the good things about this part of life when we moved from Cotter Homes, and we were bouncing around from Ms. Sharon to Jerry's house, was that I didn't have to leave my school, Shelby Elementary. I had some great teachers there, but one of them was my favorite teacher in the world: Mrs. Barrett.

Mrs. Barrett was my 4th grade teacher, and I absolutely loved her. She was a young white lady who just took a liking to me and all her students really, who were mostly black. For some reason that I couldn't understand as a kid, all the other teachers didn't like her. Now though, I think it was because she went above and beyond for her students and because she was a little well-off financially. She wasn't supposed to, but she even did things to help me outside of school.

I was a huge animal fanatic at the time, and she and her husband would pick me up to take me to the Cincinnati Zoo without asking for anything from me or my mom. Her husband was an architect, too, so he was the one who started my interest in architecture as a kid. They even let me come over to their house a few times. It was clear that they were living on the richer side of things. But the amazing thing about them was they didn't treat me like I was beneath them or anything. They were some of the kindest and most generous people I had ever met.

My whole classroom was pretty much nothing but inner-city kids who had never really traveled anywhere far away, so one day Mrs. Barrett had an idea. She had all of us draw pictures of animals from Australia, and I remember drawing a koala bear. We had no idea what it was for. So the next day, we came in, and the classroom was set up like plane seats! She had everything right: there were two seats on each side and there was an aisle down the middle. She came down the aisle with a cart serving snacks—I had never experienced anything like that before!

We acted like we were flying to Australia, and we finally landed. Then we got off the "plane," we got on the "tour bus" and went traveling through Australia on a safari learning about the different animals using the pictures we had drawn the day before.

Mrs. Barrett was always doing things like that to make school and learning fun, and 4th grade is a year that I always love remembering.

Now it's important to know when I was living in Cotter Homes, I had always been doing amazing in school. But when I got to Shelby Elementary, especially in 5th grade, when we started living with Jerry, my grades began to drop.

In the beginning part of 5th grade, I had a teacher named Ms. Sohm. I had gotten in trouble for talking all the time in class, so she moved my desk right next to hers...but I remember when the next grade reports came out, I went from a D to B, all because I had nobody to talk to. My teacher saw my grades and told me, "Well hey, Robert, you can move back to your area now."

But I was like, "Nah! I got good grades, so I'm gonna sit right here next to you!"

Even then, at a young age, I decided to make a choice that was going to make me better, even if it made me seem like I wasn't cool. So much was happening in my life that I couldn't control, but one thing I could was my grades. I wasn't used to failing, and I wasn't about to start!

For the most part, everything was going fine. But my mom started getting back on drugs, and things started changing again.

The difference this time was Camp, and I were a little

older, and we knew that our mom was on drugs. Kids at school were making jokes about crackheads, and it was in the movies that were coming out, so we knew what they meant.

One day we were at the house playing with our friends. The siding on the houses back then had this white stuff on it that would rub off on your clothes when you rubbed up against it, so when we were running between houses playing, it got on our clothes. We came into the house, and our mom was tweaking out.

"What's that on y'all? What's that?"

Me and Camp looked at each other in confusion. "What are you talking about mom, there's nothing on us!"

She ignored us and pulled us both into the bathroom and asked us, "Y'all got drugs?"

We both told her, "No, mama, no!"

Our mom still wasn't believing us, and instead, she made us strip out of all our clothes. "Y'all hiding drugs from me, y'all hiding drugs!" She was so convinced that we were hiding drugs from her, she checked our butts as if we might have stuffed something in there.

She had never done anything like that before, and I felt super, super violated. That was a real critical point that made me realize things were a lot more wrong than I had ever thought before.

The thing was, when my mom was off drugs, she was good. It was only when she got caught up in them that she started having issues. But one of the few good memories I have with her during that time is one day she wanted me to walk to the store with her. She had heard about how I was always so fast, and she said to me, "Yeah, I heard around the neighborhood that you real fast!"

That just made me swell up because even in Cotter Homes, I was always the fastest kid. I started gloating a little bit, "Yeah, yeah, yeah, mama, you know!"

So then she asked me, "You wanna race me to the store?"

She had no idea how fast I really was, and I let her know! "Mama, you don't wanna race me to the store, I'm gonna win!"

Man, my mama blew me the fuck out. She beat me so badly; I had no idea she was that fast! After she beat me that day, I never raced her again...but, I finally realized where I got my speed from!

Still though, mom kept leaving for weeks at a time, and Jerry eventually just kicked us out.

This time we found our way into a women's shelter, and that was probably one of the happier times of my young life. My mom, my brothers, and I were together, and we were in a safe place with other women and kids who were also escaping some type of situation going on in their lives. All the moms would make popcorn so the kids could eat it at night and watch movies, we had our own rooms...it was great!

Even while we were at the shelter, I was still able to go to Shelby Elementary, and I loved it because I had made friends there.

One of my boys there had started dating a girl who

was so pretty; everybody wanted to date her. But one of her friends was the girl that *nobody* wanted to date. She was taller than everybody, but because of that, and the fact that nobody wanted to date her, she kind of was a bully. And she liked *me*.

My boy came up to me one day at school and said, "Hey Rob, her friend wanna date you."

Immediately I was like, "Nah!"

But then the friend came back with, "Nah? Tell him we go together, or I'm gonna beat him up."

Wow, what the crap!

So now I found myself in a relationship with this girl. She would make me sit with them during breakfast and lunch. Then after school, I would have to walk her to a certain corner where she would turn off with her friends... it was just too much!

At this age, Camp was my hero. I had never beat him up, and because I always lost, I thought he always won because he was older. So then I figured, if you're older than somebody, you should be able to beat them up. Right?

Even though we were living in the shelter, we were still cool with Nalona and Shaneka, Jerry's daughters, and so I set out to get Shaneka to fight this girl for me. Shaneka was close to Camp's age and older than me, so I knew she would win.

I'll never forget it. It was a Friday after school that we were walking home, and we started getting close to the intersection that we would split off on. I had told Shaneka to meet us there. The girl was talking to me and making plans for next week, but as soon as I saw Shaneka, I yanked my hand out of hers (we *always* had to hold hands), yelled, "Get the fuck off me!" and took off running!

"Ahhh, yeah!" I hollered. I was standing next to Shaneka now, and I was feeling myself! "Yeah, we don't go together! Shaneka, beat her up!"

Shaneka ran across the street toward her saying, "Yeah, you messing with my little brother!"

But just as quickly as I had started feeling myself, my stomach started dropping. I couldn't believe what I was seeing. Shaneka was getting beat up.

I was watching her get her ass whooped, and I had set it up! *Oh shit*, I thought, *this ain't going how I want it to go!*

As soon as my ex-girlfriend finished beating Shaneka up, she looked dead at me. I took that as my cue to start running, but I could hear her yelling behind me, "Robert, I'm gonna get you on Monday, I'm gonna see you in school!"

But here's why God is good. That was the same day that a cop came to the shelter to pick me up and take me to another foster home. So, I never went back to that school on that Monday. God really looked out for me!

Even though the shelter was a good place to stay, our mom would still leave us there by ourselves. So we would go to school in the morning, and when we came home, she would be gone. The shelter only let that happen for so many days before they called Child Protective Services, so that same Friday when I came home from school, a cop was there waiting to take me to my new foster home.

Since Camp was in middle school, he rode a different bus home, but he never showed up that day at the shelter. So the cop took me to the home of a family called the Bethels, and I ended up spending my first night there by myself. It was the first time I had ever been apart from my brother in my life. Mrs. Bethel told me the next day that Camp did actually show up to the shelter, but when he saw the cop, he ran! They searched for him all that night and finally found him the next day, but Camp later told me he let himself get caught because he didn't want to leave me by myself.

This family, unlike the previous foster homes, was nice. The Bethels were what many would consider middle class; the wife owned a daycare center, and the husband drove trucks delivering milk. They still received money for fostering kids, but I could tell they really did it because they loved children. Not only did they use the money they received to actually take care of us, but they spent their own money on us as well, and with them already having four or five kids of their own, I know that must have been a stretch.

My brother and I got to meet their extended family, and we were treated just like we were their own children. It was probably one of the best times of my childhood. I really felt like they loved us, and if there was ever a family that I wanted to be adopted by, it was the Bethels.

I had to change schools while I was in the middle of

5th grade when I moved with the Bethels, and one day I was sitting in class when I saw Mrs. Barrett come in. I had no idea she was even at this school. She started talking to my teacher, and I wanted to yell out so bad, "Mrs. Barrett, it's me, it's me!"

What I didn't know was that she had actually been looking for me since I left the shelter and Shelby Elementary, so she was coming to get me out of my class!

Mrs. Barrett turned around and said, "Robert!" and just like that, my teacher let me go with her to her classroom. She introduced me to her class as one of her favorite students and told them how much she and her husband loved my poetry...it was so good to see her again and to know that I hadn't been forgotten.

Now, at this point, it's probably clear how much trauma I had experienced as a young boy. So, it's probably no surprise that I had a bit of an "attitude problem" when it came to some adults, but even so, I didn't really consider myself to be a "bad" kid. I really believe it was due to enduring the constant instability of what were supposed to be safe environments and unexpected behavior from adult figures who were supposed to be grounded and dependable. Having had those experiences at such an early and critical age, I developed an attitude that was meant to protect myself from being hurt again.

However my attitude came across, the Bethels still showed me love and took care of me, and I wanted to be with them. So, one day when our social worker came to visit, I stood close to a window to listen in to her talking with Mrs. Bethel outside. When I heard her bring up the topic of adopting us, I was beyond excited! And when Mrs. Bethel told her that she and her husband would love to adopt us, I felt like my world was being set back in place! I was overjoyed. A happy feeling settled over me as she described how my brother was a good kid, but my stomach dropped as she went on to say how I "had an attitude" on me.

Up to that point, I never really considered if I was a "bad" kid or not, and her words really stuck with me. I begin to think about my behavior and attitudes more than I had before, and for a long time, I felt like it was my fault we didn't get adopted by the Bethels. To this day, I never told my brother what I heard and how guilty and responsible I felt for the hard times that came afterward.

While living with the Bethels, Camp and I got to see our mom briefly, even though it was for a sad occasion. Our mom had gotten pregnant and had our little sister Latoya, but she had died a year later from medical complications she just couldn't recover from. So at her funeral, we got to see our mom, Anthony, and meet our new little brother, also named Anthony. Someone took a picture of us, all of our mom's boys standing with her, and that would be a picture I held onto for a long time.

Even though they didn't adopt us, the Bethels continued to love and care for us as their own, until we found out one day that our aunt Jackie and uncle Omar, my mom's sister and stepbrother, were in court trying to get custody of my brothers and me. I was very excited since the last time I had seen them was at the parties we used to have when we were younger. I remembered my mom and my aunt sharing laughs together, and that only reinforced a good sense of comfort and family in me.

All I could think of was how I was going to be with my actual family again, and how much they must already care for us if they were going so far as to fight for custody of us in court. I was happy to see my cousins, whom I hadn't seen in a long time, and I could already picture how much fun we were going to have, all living together under one roof. And since overhearing Mrs. Bethel say I had an attitude problem, it felt even more right to go back to live with my real family.

My aunt and uncle did eventually win custody of my brothers and me. But moving in with them started one of the most terrible periods in my life.

THE GRUDGE

My uncle Omar and aunt Jackie won custody of me and my brothers, Camp and Anthony, right in the middle of my 6th grade year, and we stayed with them all the way up to the middle of my 8th grade year. While life started to change for the better for me at school, those two years were still one of the worst times of my life.

When people think of family, they never think of people who will hurt them; most of the time, we think of home, comfort, and safety. And I had always heard as a kid, "Live with your family, 'cause that's family!'"

That's exactly along the lines of what I was expecting with my aunt and uncle: a warm welcome back with open arms. But we got the exact opposite. What made it all so crazy was that the memories I had of uncle Omar, aunt Jackie, and my cousins were nothing but happy ones, and I had seen them just a few years before.

Back when we lived with Herman, there were a lot of

house parties, and I can remember seeing my uncle and aunt there. I guess it's easy to figure that people are good as long as you only really see them in good times, but I didn't know any better as a kid. In particular, I could clearly remember watching my mom and Aunt Jackie laughing together, so I just naturally assumed she was that type of person: happy, friendly, and someone who loved my mom.

But those memories of them couldn't have been any farther away from my new reality. Living with them was even worse than living with Ms. Jackson. Aunt Jackie and Uncle Omar treated my brothers and me like we were regular foster kids instead of family. That hurt the most, especially with just coming from a home like the Bethels, where they actually wanted us.

I didn't know how at the time, but Aunt Jackie and Uncle Omar somehow managed to work the system so that they were able to foster us and still get paid by the state, even though we were all family. As if that wasn't shady enough, unlike the Bethels, they didn't even spend the money they were getting on us, much less their own money. One of the worst parts of living there was the abuse me and my brothers had to endure.

But things didn't start breaking down right away, and for the first few weeks that we were with them, I actually thought Uncle Omar and Aunt Jackie were pretty well-off. They had this really wack-looking green station wagon that was just plain embarrassing to be seen in, but at least they had a car, right? And coming from the Bethels in my 6th grade year, me and my brothers still had pretty decent clothes from them, so we weren't too concerned about anything at first. But as time went by, we started realizing that our uncle and aunt didn't have things as well put together as we thought.

If you counted me, my brothers, my cousins, my uncle, and my aunt, there were nine of us living in the house altogether. But the house only had one bedroom! Their house was a shotgun house, too: if you opened the front door, you could look all the way straight through to the back door. The one-bedroom in the house was upstairs, and that was where all five of us boys slept in a set of bunk beds and then another standalone bed. The two girls slept in the family room downstairs on a pullout couch where the TV was, and Uncle Omar and Aunt Jackie stayed in what was supposed to be the living room but became their private bedroom. There was also a bathroom downstairs, a bathroom upstairs, a kitchen, and that was it.

Watching Aunt Jackie and Uncle Omar, trying to figure them out, I started noticing that they were heavy drinkers and weed users. I wasn't too sure if they did any other type of strong drugs, but I knew for a fact they smoked weed because my aunt Jackie had her own little plants she would grow out in the front garden. It seemed pretty bold to me, but I guess she figured if she grew it right there with all the other flowers and plants, nobody would really notice!

Where we stayed was right on the border of Portland and West Louisville, so literally all the black people lived on one side of the street, all the white people lived on the other side of the street, and we were right in the middle. So when I went to Western Middle School, I would avoid it as best as I could, but I would always hear about some type of racial fight breaking out. All of the kids would still play with each other in the neighborhood though, because we weren't thinking about any of the stuff our parents thought about. But as soon as our parents would come out, somebody would make us stop or come inside.

Across the street from us were also some other white families that lived bunched up in a group of townhouses, but they were very racist and even more into drugs and alcohol than my aunt and uncle, so we didn't play with them at all. As far as I knew, my family was the only black family that was in this area with all these white families, and the pressure was high.

One night I heard a bunch of commotion outside, and I ran to my window to hear what was going on. Down in the road below, some of the people from the white family across the street were chasing another guy who was mixed who had been hanging around the neighborhood. I was confused why they were chasing him because I had seen them all hanging out with each other before, but then I heard one of them call out, "Go get with your nigger lover mom, she's a nigger lover!"

This was the first time I had really seen any racism up close, and I was honestly a little bit in disbelief. I had kind of encountered it with Ms. Jackson and people of my own race, but I had never seen this type of blatant racism from one group of people towards another.

The wild thing about it was the guy wasn't even really trying to leave; he just kept running around apologizing and begging them to accept him, while they kept chasing him trying to catch him and beat him up. I sat there in my window looking at the whole thing thinking, *Wow, this stuff really happens.* They had all been cool before, but as soon as they found out his mom was dating a black guy, they flipped the script on him. It was crazy to me!

Moving from the Bethels to my auntie and uncle's house was giving me a culture shock on every level, from the racism that I was now seeing and experiencing, to the way that we were living at home.

The first time I ever went digging through other people's trash was because of them. People would put their old furniture, clothes, and stuff on the side of the road, and we would go riding around in that ugly station wagon, park right on the street, and get out to see what we could find to use at home. If we weren't digging through people's stuff on the street, we were going to the DAV thrift shop and bringing huge trash bags of clothes home, dumping it out on the bed, and sifting through it to see what we could fit.

They never tried to buy us anything new...but it was nothing for Aunt Jackie and Uncle Omar to spend money on alcohol, weed, and have adult parties all the time.

When I started to grow out of the clothes I had as I went into 7th grade, I started having to wear the clothes we were getting from these different places, and it just made going to school tougher. Things were so rough; Camp started cutting our hair so we wouldn't look too bad. I was already kind of seen as the nerdy black kid, and now I was the nerdy, bummy, black kid who was going around digging through trash. I didn't want to give anybody any more ammunition to rag on me at school. So every chance I could avoid being seen with my family, I did, even if it meant me walking home instead of getting a ride in a doody green station wagon!

Somehow in all of this, Camp still seemed to be pretty popular. I don't know what he was doing that was extra special, but people were still coming by to try to fight him! Even though I was getting made fun of, I still wasn't much of a fighter, but Camp didn't let it stop him. A bunch of guys from the Beecher Terrace and Village West area would always come to the house to try to fight him. Camp would get into it with these dudes everyone called 'the twins' and a guy named Junkyard all the time.

But besides people coming by to fight, we never had too much excitement because we weren't allowed to go anywhere. The only time we ever got to leave the house besides going to school was if my uncle decided to take us fishing. Outside of that, we could only do one of three things: stay inside, go in the backyard, or go in the alley that was right beside the house.

This was the first time I started getting interested in basketball though, because we had all watched the NBA playoff series where it was Michael Jordan and the Bulls versus Magic Johnson and the Lakers. Jordan had done that crazy move where he switched the ball between his hands when he was in the air, and that made me want to play even more! With such a limited environment, we had to get creative, so all of us kids nailed a crate up to a telephone pole in the alley to play basketball, and it worked!

Outside of being in the house or the alley, one thing that we did get to do was join a boys' choir at a local church.

At first, I didn't know why we were suddenly allowed to join and go to all the practices and concerts. We did lots of cool stuff, like making an album and sing with the Harlem Boys Choir. When I got older and realized just how big the Harlem Boys Choir was, it made perfect sense why he let us join back then: Uncle Omar probably thought there was going to be a check involved.

The thing about Uncle Omar was he was always kind of scammerish, like a con artist. If he wasn't getting something out of a situation, he wasn't doing it, and he wasn't going to let us do it. But as soon as he heard what that choir was doing, as long as it involved possibly getting some money, he was rushing to get us involved!

We would go there once a week, and then we would sing at church on Sundays. But the one thing I did like my uncle for on Sundays was he would act like we were hungry so that we could leave early. He wasn't trying to sit there for three hours after we were done singing!

Uncle Omar was a strict, strict man who thought discipline was the most important thing for a kid, so he would make us all chop wood constantly as if that was the solution. Really, it was probably just because they had an old school fire oven that only ran on wood, and he didn't want to chop wood himself, but according to him, it was giving us "structure." He made sure that he instilled fear in us, and we respected him just because we were too afraid to do anything else.

Our life at home was generally horrible, so we'd all play these fantasy games of how we wanted things to be. There was a 'house of the week' ad in the paper, and looking forward to each new house is actually what started my love of architecture. My brothers, cousins, and I would get the weekly newspaper, go through it, and pick out all the things we wanted in our life: nice houses, cars, groceries, shoes.

Around this time, Jordans and Bo Jacksons were coming out, and we'd fantasize about getting those so much that we started drawing pictures of them. Camp was this amazing artist, and watching him draw made me want to learn too, so I did. When we weren't outside playing, the only other thing we could do was be inside, so we spent that time drawing. We didn't just keep the pictures for ourselves though; we would give them to our youngest cousin so he could sell them at his elementary school for 25 cents apiece.

Now, the more they started selling, the more we started jazzing them up. We'd shave off little pieces of crayon and glue it to the paper to give it this 3D effect, so now they weren't just looking at a picture, they could actually feel the shoe!

Things were going pretty good with our art operation

until one day, Aunt Jackie happened to get a passing look at our crayons and saw that a few were a little shaved down.

"Who's wasting all these crayons?"

We were all confused, and we tried to explain that we weren't wasting anything, we were selling pictures. We were young entrepreneurs! But she wasn't hearing it, and she whooped all our asses. Then to make it worse, she told us when Uncle Omar got home, she was going to tell him what we were doing and get him to whoop our asses too!

By this point, Camp had stopped drawing pictures because he had gotten a job. It was really just me drawing and selling them, so he was determined not to get whooped for something he wasn't doing! Aunt Jackie and Uncle Omar were the types where if one of us got in trouble, they were whooping all of us, but Camp wasn't hearing it this time.

When Uncle Omar came home and tried to catch him, Camp ended up running out of the house to our grandmother's house, and I was amazed! They figured out where he went pretty quickly just because there wasn't really anywhere else we could go in town, but as a kid, I was in awe of him thinking, *Wow, how'd he know how to get over there to grandmama's house?*

Camp still got his ass whooped when they brought him back, but I remember Uncle Omar talking to him in the living room and basically just shitting on my mom. He was trying to make it seem like he and Aunt Jackie were doing us a favor by taking care of us, and Camp was just causing trouble and making things hard. It was a lame attempt at brainwashing because that was the furthest thing from the truth.

All of us were treated badly, and we would get whoopings for doing little to nothing, but my little brother Anthony was the one who really got the brunt of a lot of the abuse. Uncle Omar would make him do things that you would expect to hear from someone in the military telling stories like he was some type of deranged drill sergeant, and my brother was a disrespectful soldier who was asking for it.

Anthony was only in kindergarten at the time, so there wasn't even much trouble he could get into, but Uncle Omar seemed to make it his mission in life to torture him. He would beat Anthony with extension cords so badly that he would be dripping blood, and the flesh would literally be hanging from his body.

When I got older and watched *The Passion of the Christ,* it hit home for me in a way I didn't expect...because the way those soldiers were beating Jesus, to the point where gruesome chunks of flesh were being ripped and hanging from his body, reminded me just how Uncle Omar used to beat Anthony. Even to this day, after another foster mom rubbed him down with cocoa butter to try to heal his wounds, Anthony still has scars from those beatings from when he was five years old.

The whole situation was just too much for my young mind! How could these people who were my blood family, really not seem to care about or even love us? Even Ms.

Robie, our first foster mom, who was so cold and distant, didn't abuse us like this!

I was so scared, especially as a young boy, because here was a man who was supposed to be taking care of us. It was terrifying, but still, looking back, I wish I would have stood up to Uncle Omar.

On top of the physical abuse, Uncle Omar and Aunt Jackie were always trying to put our cousins and us against each other. This made me resent them even more because I genuinely didn't have anything against my cousins; I really did love them! All I wanted was for us to get along and have good times with each other like regular kid cousins do: running outside together, staying up late, getting in trouble, but still having each other's backs. Instead, my cousins started to resent us just for even being there, especially me, as I kept on doing well in school.

The funny thing was, I wasn't even trying all that hard to prove anything to anybody. Before I got to their house, I was already a pretty good student, but I had really started focusing on school out of fear and to try to find something else to put my mind on. If things hadn't been so bad at home, I might not have started excelling like I did in middle school. Outside of all the attention I was getting at school, all I was really thinking on any given day when school was over was, *Great; now I gotta go home and deal with this shit.*

Around this time, I had watched Denzel Washington in the movie *Mo' Better Blues*, and I really wanted to play the trumpet. So, I went to Uncle Omar to ask him to sign me up for the program they had just started at school, and he promised me he would do it.

"I'ma let you play, I'ma let you play."

But he never did, because my cousin was already playing the clarinet so he could start learning the saxophone, and music was just another area that Uncle Omar didn't want me to outshine my cousins. He could never give me a good reason why he couldn't sign the paperwork, especially since the program was free! He just didn't want me to add to my accomplishments.

In any case, somehow, I just found my groove and kept doing well. I started getting attention and became something like a celebrity in Western Middle School and my city. I met the governor of Kentucky, the Board of Education actually asked me (a young kid!) to start a club, limos were picking me up from the house so I could go hang out with the governor's son at a football game.

One time, I even won an award for a writing contest with an essay that was all about my uncle. The crazy thing about it? The whole story was a straight-up lie. We had to write about someone we knew, and what we thought about them, so I told this story about how he was an architect, and how I wanted to be just like him and all these things that just were not true. I did fear my uncle Omar, but definitely not in a healthy way, and I didn't admire him at all. But at this point in my life, I was just trying to do anything I could to distract myself from the hell that was at home.

It was unbelievable how these different doors were opening up for me...just as crazy as the fact that I was living this amazing type of life out in public with people who really didn't know me, but I was being abused and humiliated in private by family who was supposed to love me.

You would think all this would have been enough to get at least my uncle Omar and aunt Jackie to lighten up on the abuse, but this kind of backfired on me and started causing even more problems for me at home. Every time I brought home a report card with good grades or told my family about some type of recognition I had received for another activity, my uncle Omar would get even more upset!

He would go off on one cousin in particular about how he needed to step up their game and keep up with me. It was like he was saying, "How is the crack baby kid gonna be better than my kid?" And of course, even though it wasn't my fault, my cousins started to hate me for it, and it always felt like we were in competition with each other.

Still, I managed to keep my head on straight and stayed focused. It was during this period in my life when one area seemed to be getting better while another area was getting steadily worse, that I would see my mom again. And I didn't know it then, but it was the last time I would ever get to see her.

One day my brothers and I were at home with our cousins while our aunt and uncle were out and about. I heard someone knocking at the door downstairs, and Camp went down first to answer it since he was the oldest. I stayed upstairs for a minute, thinking it was probably just another Jehovah's Witness or someone like that until I realized he was still downstairs after a short while.

Wondering what was taking him so long, I went down the steps and heard a woman's voice. Turning the corner, I come face to face with my mom, and she calls out, "Oh my God, Mone, come here!" So I run to her, and we're all hugging and kissing each other, having been apart for so long. She's looking at us, saying, "How y'all doing? Oh, y'all look so good!" and we're just soaking it all up. By this time, my cousins have heard us at the door, so they've come downstairs too, and my mom's just as happy to see them.

We're basically having a mini family reunion at the door, but it's short-lived because, after only a few minutes of my mom showing up, my aunt and uncle pulled right up in the yard.

They saw my mom, and before the car was even in park, Aunt Jackie jumped out. "Get the fuck away from my door. I'll call the police right now!" she was screaming. Aunt Jackie is running up the sidewalk while my mom is begging her, "Please, please, just let me see my kids," but it was like she was deaf to everything my mom was trying to say.

One thing nobody would do was run up on my mom because she was a fighter. Even though Aunt Jackie was bigger than my mom, I think she still knew it wouldn't be wise to try to put her hands on her, so cussing and making a big scene was the next closest thing.

At this point, my mom has tears streaming down her

face, still begging my aunt Jackie to just let her see us while Uncle Omar walks past us inside the house to do something, probably to call the police. Camp and I are still standing at the front door, but now we're crying and watching in shock as Aunt Jackie is cussing my mom out and threatening her with the police to get her to leave.

For a long time, I wondered what could have possibly happened between my mom and Aunt Jackie to make her hate my mom so much. Like I said in the beginning, Uncle Omar and Aunt Jackie used to come to our place in Cotter Homes and have a good time at the parties. I only ever saw my mom and Aunt Jackie laughing and smiling with each other, so to see her cussing my mom out like this was shocking. What could make two sisters fall out like that? But I started to figure when I got older, it was probably a dude, and that maybe my mom had slept with my uncle Omar when she was going in and out. Mom was always the more attractive, hourglass figure type of woman, and it didn't seem too hard to believe that something like that could have happened. It just made sense with the way my aunt Jackie suddenly hated my mom and everything about her, while my uncle Omar just kind of avoided the whole situation.

When I thought about it even more, my theory made sense, especially if Anthony was actually my uncle Omar's son, because even though all three of us would get whoop-ings, Anthony *always* got it worse. I don't remember my aunt Jackie whooping him that much, but the way Uncle Omar would whoop and torture him made it seem like he was taking out his personal feelings on him...or like he trying to prove to my aunt that he didn't cheat, or something.

Nothing else really makes sense to explain why they treated all of us so bad, and why my aunt Jackie suddenly hated my mom, to the point where she wouldn't even let her sister see her kids.

The people that had brought my mom there were still sitting in the alley on the side of the house waiting for her, and they walked up trying to get her to leave before things got too out of hand. I remember feeling so much hatred for my aunt Jackie in that moment because the last time I had seen my mom was at Latoya's funeral about three years before. It wasn't even a thought that this would be the last time I would see my mom, and the last memory I have of her is seeing her crying and reaching out for us in the back-seat of that car as they drove away.

If there was any hope in me of Uncle Omar and Aunt Jackie maybe still having some good deep down in them towards us at this point, it was all destroyed in this moment. I had been seeing all this time that they were on some Dr. Jekyll/Mr. Hyde shit and this right here really drove the point home. They flipped when they wanted to without thinking about anybody else but themselves, and I learned the hard way from them that people aren't always who they present themselves to be.

Hate had already started to build in me from how they were abusing us, but after this, I made up in my mind that

I was done with them. I would never forgive them, no matter what anybody said to me.

Things only got worse for us at their house after this, and the next time I saw my mom, she was in a casket. It would be a long time before I was able to talk to Uncle Omar and Aunt Jackie about just how badly what they did affected me.

NEVER AGAIN

Like I said in the last chapter, during middle school, I really started to hit my stride. Before, Camp had seemed to outshine me not just in terms of our attitudes, but also in academics. But as we got older, it was like we started swapping places: the more I started focusing on school, the more he started focusing on other things. We had always been close, but this small change in our dynamic would begin to pull us in opposite directions.

Even though that was going on, we were still living with my uncle Omar and aunt Jackie and were determined to make it out of there. I was going strong in school in 8th grade, doing my best to the point that high schools had started to compete with each other to get me to come to their school, and my brother had just started working his first job. With my increased number of activities and my brother's new job, both of us weren't at the house as much as we used to be, and that meant Camp, and I weren't always able to be there to keep an eye out for Anthony like we were used to.

So one Saturday morning, everybody was busy. I was at the Whitney Young Scholars group at school (a program that promised to eventually pay for college if you stayed involved with them), Camp was at work, my uncle and aunt had gone fishing, and the rest of my cousins and Anthony were left at home alone. We all knew that we weren't allowed to leave the house without permission, especially when no adults were at home, but on that day, for some reason, my cousins decided that they were going to the store to get snacks.

To get where they were going, they had to cross a four-lane street: two lanes going in one direction, two lanes going in the other. My oldest cousin darted out first, even though traffic was coming. Then, the remaining cousins started running across the street one by one. Since everyone else was taking off across the street, Anthony took off right after them. When the cousins saw him and realized traffic was coming straight towards him, they tried to wave to him to go back, but it was too late. Anthony hesitated in the middle of the street, and by the time he turned around, he was hit by a car.

The police and paramedics showed up, but all my cousins got scared, so they ran and left Anthony there alone. Since there were no adults around, they ended up having to take a closer look to figure out where he lived and who he was, and that's when they discovered all the scars he had on his body. When I got back home from

Whitney Young Scholars, I found out everything that had happened, and that's how the authorities finally got involved in our case. We were taken out of their home within a week or so while they kept Anthony in the hospital to treat him, but it seemed like one of the longest weeks of my life.

Now, everyone in my family knew that I looked just like my mom. So the whole time we lived with them, my uncle Omar and aunt Jackie seemed to make it a point to single me out because of that simple fact. One time my cousin went missing, and while trying to figure out what could've happened, Aunt Jackie accused *me*, "Ramone probably did it."

Out of seven kids in the house, all I could think was, *why would you pick me?* There was no reason even to think I had anything to do with it; I had never done anything but do good in school. But they knew how much I didn't like them, and that made me the easy target for them to place the blame for anything on.

A lot of my family also said I had an attitude like my mom, which pissed them off to no end, but I think it was more that I just wasn't good at hiding my feelings. If someone said something that was a straight-up lie or they treated us badly but tried to act like everything was good, I wasn't the kid who would smile with them to keep up appearances. I was a good kid who didn't want any trouble, but I wasn't about to be fake about anything just to keep the peace. I tried to respect Uncle Omar and Aunt Jackie as adults the best I could, but being picked on so much for nothing really put a deep hatred in me, and I guess it just showed up to others as a bad attitude.

So in that last week, before we left their house, it seemed like whatever little thing I could get in trouble for, I got in trouble for.

One day me, my younger cousin Ali, and my older cousin, whom Uncle Omar had pushed to compete with me, were all in our room doing our separate things when suddenly Ali yelled, "Mone, watch out!"

I spun around to see my cousin standing over me with a big piece of wood gripped between his hands and raised high over his head, about to smash it down on the back of my head. Before I could even really process what was happening, I shot my hands out to grab the wood, snatched it out of his hand, and threw it down to the side. I looked at him in disbelief and shouted, "Oh, so you trying to kill me!"

I grabbed my cousin by his neck, slung him down on the bed, and started choking him as I pressed him into the bed. All I could keep repeating was, "You trying to kill me, dude? You trying to kill me?"

Not even five seconds passed before Aunt Jackie walked into the room, and immediately she went into defense mode. "Get off my baby!" she screamed.

She grabbed me off of him, and while she's looking over him to make sure he's OK, I tried to explain what was really going on, "He tried to hit me with..."

But she didn't care about none of that and wasn't trying to hear anything I was trying to say. And at this point, I'm mad because the way she responded was just showing me that they really didn't give a fuck about me. My cousin was trying to beat my head in with a piece of wood, and to them, it was OK. Aunt Jackie was giving me hell because my hands were around his neck after he almost hurt me...but I wasn't even trying to really hurt him. I just wanted to defend myself!

So now, whether I'm at the house or I'm at school, I'm walking around with an attitude. I'm not speaking to anybody, and I don't care anymore.

Within a few days of this happening, Aunt Jackie and Uncle Omar called me downstairs one night and handed me the phone.

I had no idea who it was, but I wasn't raised to be disrespectful to adults at all, so I just said, "Hello?"

"Mone, what are you doing over there?"

Still clueless, I responded, "Hello? Who is this?"

"This is your uncle Beaver."

It turned out to be my mom's brother, who had been left in Alabama by my granddad. I had only met him maybe once or twice, years ago when my mom and Herman were together and throwing parties, and at that time, it was all smiles, of course. All the family was coming through regularly then. But when everything started going sideways, all the family visits disappeared. So, I hadn't heard from this guy in years.

Uncle Omar and Aunt Jackie, on the other hand, had a good relationship with Uncle Beaver. They had gone to Alabama plenty of times with their kids, so they all knew each other well, but me and my brothers had never gone up there to visit. Having not seen him since I was in the 1st or 2nd grade, I really didn't have any idea who he was.

Without knowing the situation at all, he had taken their side of the story and was on the phone trying to discipline me. "What you doing, man? 'Cause you don't want me coming there and..."

I don't even remember the rest of what he said because I literally looked at the phone, threw it down, and just walked off. It was the first time in my life that I had ever disrespected an adult on purpose. *Who was this guy to even try to talk to me like that? I didn't know him, and he definitely didn't know me,* and it just made me even madder that he had no idea what was going on, but was still trying to talk to me like he knew.

Walking off, I could hear my aunt pick the phone back up and egg on the drama even more, "Yeah, yeah, you see? He just like Donna, he just like Donna!"

I was scared of Aunt Jackie and Uncle Omar for the way they used to beat us, but in that particular moment, I just didn't care. My attitude had become, *I Don't Give A Fuck.*

So much had happened: they had sent my mom away, my little brother had gotten hit by a car, we had been beaten almost every day for nothing—

That day for me was a Fuck-With-Me-If-You-Want day. If they thought I was like my mom so bad, they were going to see just how true it was if they kept on messing with me. Usually, I would have never done something like that because I was scared of the consequences, but I just didn't care. I wasn't afraid of them anymore. What else could they possibly do to me?

Luckily, the next day, we left out of their house.

I used to wonder how Aunt Jackie and Uncle Omar were able to get away with all the crazy stuff they did to us and still avoid any type of punishment when our social worker would come over. In the beginning of living there, I figured out that our young social worker at the time who put us in their home was actually somehow related to our uncle. Or at least, Uncle Omar conned his way into making her think that. He was such a smooth talker, even though he probably didn't even know her at all. He made her think since they must have known the same people, he must have been a good guy. As soon as we were officially placed in their home, she completely looked the other way for those two years.

We were able to get a new social worker who wasn't connected to my family in any way, but this time we were put into different homes. I was placed into a home with a man named Derek, and my brother Camp was put into the home of Derek's mom, Ms. Ramsey. This was the first time in our lives that we had not lived together.

You might think we weren't completely separated since our foster parents were related. But the only other time I had ever not been with Camp was that first night at the Bethels' house. We actually didn't live too far away from each other at this point, but us not being under the same roof together really changed our relationship forever.

The closeness that we once had, we never got back, even to this day.

On my end, Derek seemed to be a nice guy with a nice house, and things were already looking better within just the first few days of being there. We were coming back from seeing his mom in that first week when Uncle Omar showed up unexpectedly.

We had just walked in and didn't even have the lights on in the house yet when my uncle knocked at the door. I had walked to my room already but could hear my uncle's voice, and Derek called me out there to the front. Uncle Omar seemed to gather his courage and said, "Man, I just wanna tell you something."

In my mind, I was thinking they were trying to get us back, or he was trying to get me to say something to help them since my little brother was still in the hospital with a broken leg. As unlikely as it would have been, I thought maybe Uncle Omar was even trying to apologize. There was nothing that could have prepared me for what he was about to say.

When he told me my mother had been killed, it felt like someone froze me. I was in shock, and I remember wondering if something was wrong with me because I didn't cry right away.

The thought just kept going through my mind: I was never going to see my mom again.

Right away, Derek got me in his car, and we drove over to his mom's house to tell Camp. They weren't there, and we had to wait for them to come home. While we were sitting there on her front porch steps, Derek turned to me and said, "You know, Rob, I know I kind of just met you, but I've always prayed for a son. I know it's been a week, but I think you're great. And as unfortunate as this is, I know you just lost your mom, but you just gained a dad. If you wouldn't mind, man, I would love to adopt you as my son."

That meant a lot to me, and I took him at his word. From that point on, Derek wasn't a foster parent to me, he was my dad.

Still though, all I wanted was to be with my mom! It seemed like it was impossible for us to be together in life, and no matter what, everything that could keep us apart seemed to win. I started to become suicidal, and I looked for ways that someone could kill me so that I could go be with her.

At that time, I would walk to my grandma's house to watch my little cousin Joe, Uncle Joe's son, Derek didn't mind. She lived in a rough part of Louisville called Victory Park off 22nd Street on Grand Avenue, and everybody knew that area was where all the gangs camped out. One night I left her house to walk home, and I stood on the sidewalk across the street from one of their houses and started cussing them out like I had lost my mind. I wanted to make them mad, so every cuss word and insult I could think of, I started screaming at them at the top of my lungs. I hoped so bad that one of them would get pissed off at me and just shoot me to death. I felt like there was nothing else for me to live for, so why not just end it now?

Instead, they just looked at me like, "What the fuck is wrong with that little kid?" and kept on going about their business.

I kept doing crazy stuff like that for a few days, not thinking of anything else but dying. But a couple of days later, I was sitting on the top of my bunk bed at home in Derek's apartment by myself when I started crying uncontrollably. It was like the part of me that had been frozen finally broke suddenly, and I just couldn't stop crying. All this anger flooded my mind. I was mad at the world and kept thinking, *why did it have to happen to my mom?* I was angry at the guy who killed her, who was just some nineteen-year-old kid.

While I was sitting there, I thought about my mom and one of the conversations we had when I was younger. She had asked me what I wanted to be when I got older, and I was so young, I didn't know what it was actually called, but I told her I wanted to be one of those "train guys."

"A tra—you mean a conductor, baby?" she had corrected me.

"Yeah, that!" I remember saying.

But as I sat there remembering that conversation, I thought about how she would want me to be better and to be successful, and I knew I wouldn't do that if I kept on doing the suicidal things I was doing. I decided that night that I was going to change and honor my mom.

There was still so much anger inside of me, and I had to go to school that Monday, but no one really knew what was going on except for my language arts teacher. She came up to me in class, told me she heard about a woman who got murdered over the weekend and asked if she was related to me because our last names were similar. I told her it was my mom, and she was immediately concerned and understanding. She told me that if I just wanted to sit in class that day and not do much, it was fine.

So I went back and sat at my desk in my group with two other people, my best friend Anthony Grundy and another Larona. Me and Anthony were tight and used to joke with each other a lot, and so he started pushing my binder off the desk onto the floor over and over, and I just told him, "Ant, man, I just don't feel like playing today, can you stop? Man, my mom just died."

I don't know if he thought I was joking, but he said something back to me like, "So?"

It was like he was saying who cares, and I literally just lost it. I got up, walked around our desks, and just started swinging on him. All the rage and frustration I had was coming through every punch I landed, and it took my teacher coming over to us to pull me off of him.

After that fight, me and Anthony were never the same. We were polite to each other, but we were never best friends again.

Even though I was angry, my grades didn't suffer. I had already been a good student, and now I was determined to be better for my mom, so my mind was focused when it came to school.

Living with Derek helped a lot because he lived in

Hampton Place in the West End. It was way calmer than the side of town my aunt and uncle lived in. Also, since I was now rated as the number one middle school student in the whole city, and I was focusing on becoming great like my mom wanted for me, it felt like the sky was the limit academically.

I was relieved when Derek started buying me stuff no foster parent had ever bought me before: name-brand jogging suits, Nike shoes, all the school supplies I needed! Even though I had been doing well in school, up to this point, I still hadn't had the style I wanted. School was one of those places as a kid where you know somebody's going to talk about you real bad when you look crazy, so this dramatic change in my look boosted my self-esteem and shot my popularity through the roof!

My popularity with other kids was taking off, my reputation with the Board of Education was set, and *high schools* were falling all over themselves to get me to commit to their school. And now, after a terrible two years with Uncle Omar and Aunt Jackie, I found myself in a foster home with a father who seemed to really care about me, and even love me.

Things had been pretty terrible up to this point, and I had just suffered the loss of my mom, but it seemed like when I remembered my mom's wish for me, and I started to focus my mind on being better, that things were finally trying to work themselves out for my good.

Hearing Derek tell me he had never had a kid like me, and he wanted to adopt me as his son so soon after taking me into his house felt like a huge step in the right direction for once.

At the same time that I started to look at life differently, my brother seemed to never recover. I often look back now and see how my mom's death was like a spinning top we both got stuck on, but I came out in one direction, and Camp came out in another. Camp seemed never to bounce back, and our relationship became even more estranged. I saw him at our mom's funeral, and I would still see him every now and then at Derek's mom's house, but the tightness we once had as brothers just wasn't there anymore.

A couple of months after my mom had passed, one day, I was out and decided to go down to Ms. Ramsey's house to see Camp and spend some time with him. He was hanging out with some of his friends at one of their houses, and when I showed up, he introduced me to everybody, and we headed down to the basement to play spades.

I had played spades a few times but wasn't too familiar with the game, so I didn't know too much about the rules. We were playing and I had reneged, and one of Camp's friends caught me. I didn't know how serious it was because I didn't really care; all I was trying to do was spend time with my brother in whatever way I could, even if it meant playing a game I had no idea about!

It turned out to be a bigger deal than I thought because immediately Camp started going off on me and disrespecting me in front of his friends. This was the moment that I realized something was seriously wrong with me and Camp's relationship.

I started apologizing, but he wouldn't hear any of it.

"Man, my bad, I'm sorry—"

"Nah, man, nah, fuck that! You need to fucking leave, man, get the fuck out of here!"

I was in shock, thinking, *wait, what?*

Camp told me to leave, and I just couldn't figure out what happened to make him talk to me like that. I was his little brother, and he had never cussed me out! He had always protected me and was like a superhero to me, but he completely flipped out on me in front of his friends over this one game of spades that I knew nothing about.

I walked out of his friend's house and almost thirty blocks home, crying the whole way. *Who was this person?* I didn't remember him ever being that way, and I couldn't figure out what he might have been trying to prove to his friends that would make him treat me like shit.

From that point on, I knew things just wouldn't be the same anymore.

I never said anything to anybody about what happened, but I just said to myself, *well fuck it, he's just not my brother anymore.* He made me feel like I was just some random neighborhood kid, and I told myself I would never let him hurt me that way again. We grew apart so much that we didn't even go to each other's high school graduations, even though we were living in the same city.

I missed Camp really bad, but his absence, both physically and emotionally, forced me to grow up into being my own person instead of being a shadow of who he was. When we were younger, I looked up to him and thought the world of him. I always tried to be like him, especially when others said he was the kid they wanted. But the more I grew and started developing my own personality and goals, the more I saw the difference in the directions Camp and I were heading in. Now that he was living on the side of town that was definitely rougher than the side I was on, it wasn't too long before he started getting involved with crowds that were rougher as well.

So now me and Camp officially weren't talking anymore. Anthony Grundy, my former best friend, was not my friend anymore. That sucked a lot because we had been a basketball duo since 6th grade when I was living with Uncle Omar and Aunt Jackie. We were so good, the school even wanted us to play for the team, but I couldn't because of my uncle.

But now that we weren't friends, I started getting real close to a dude named Andrew McCubbins. He was new to the school, and me and him started hanging out together, all the time. Then his dad died not too long after my mom was killed, so we also had that in common, and it made our friendship even stronger.

Andrew had two brothers, and there was a park right down the street from Hampton Place, so we started playing basketball. Me and Andrew got so good as a team, playing other people two on two, that we would be hustling people! We were so on point; we would actually beat adults and everything.

That whole summer after 8th grade, I was living the life! I was getting a $5 allowance from Derek every week, and it was everything to me. And even though my $5 only went so far, it didn't matter too much because Andrew's mom was giving him money from his dad's social security check, and he was paying for stuff for both of us some-times...so we weren't struggling to get anything we really wanted as young teenagers. We were hanging out every day, looking good and not doing anything but talking to girls and going girl-crazy!

Even though I had lost my mom and taken a lot of losses in a short time, for the first time in a long time, life was better.

4

DISRESPECT

Here I was, still at the beginning of my 8th grade year. I was finally in a home where I was wanted, and it seemed like the sky was the limit! All through 7th grade up to now, I had been in charge of programs, I had been winning lots of awards for my school, and my reputation with everyone (teachers, the Board of Education, high schools) was on a whole 'nother level. When my school would go on trips, they would literally give me my own room, when even teachers had to share two to a room!

And now, unlike with Uncle Omar, I was living with a man who was genuinely proud of me and wanted to see me do well. Derek was just about the closest thing to a father I'd had in a long time, and he showed it by the way he supported me. Past buying me all the freshest clothes, shoes, and all that stuff, we had grown close and actually developed a relationship. Derek had other kids he was fostering at his house while I was living there, but out of all of us, he started calling me his son, and that made me feel wanted for the first time in a long time.

So I was finally experiencing what it was like to be wanted and celebrated at home, and it was just fitting right in with what was happening at school. Like I said before, all the high schools in Louisville were starting to come after me since it was the summer before 9th grade, but I guess I just started to get a little too comfortable with the attention because I started to drag my feet on making a choice. This became a problem because the high schools in the area were all kind of program-specific; if you wanted to focus on making music or maybe engineering as a potential career, there were different schools with programs that focused mainly on those subjects.

At that time, I wanted to be an architect, and there was a particular school called Doss that I really wanted to go to because I knew they had the perfect architectural program. But again, it was summertime before my 9th grade year started, and I was just having too much fun!

The letters from all these schools were piling up like they were inviting a celebrity's kid to be the new face of their school, but to my young mind, which was now used to being ran after, I figured I had all the time in the world. I was too busy living my best young life with Andrew over the summer!

The problem I didn't know I had yet was the city was transitioning from having its high schools being predominantly black or white, so the year I was starting 9th grade was the year they were making schools integrate. That meant that there were different quotas they had to meet, but when they reached it, they weren't letting any more students in.

Summer started winding down, and when I finally started getting on to picking a high school, it was too late. Derek took me to Doss High (my dream school at this point) to apply, but when I got there, I was told I had waited too long to start the new school year with them. The principal told me I could still apply, but I would have to wait until the second semester before there would be any spots open for me to get in, and I was pissed! I started flipping out, hollering, "Do you know who I am? I'm friends with the governor and his son, do you know the governor and his son? I can call them right now!" It took Derek pulling me out of there to really calm me down.

My young pride was hurt, but we went to Central High School next, my second choice in the city. They told me the same thing: they'd been sending me letters for a while and hadn't heard anything back from me, so I had to wait until next semester for a chance to get in. This time, I lost it. "I'm the best kid in this city, number one, you *need* me at this school! *Do you know who I am?*"

It's crazy how entitled I thought I was at thirteen years old. I legit thought I could bully these people into letting me into their school on my own time. Even though I was the number one kid in the city, and I had gotten used to having all these different perks, I forgot I still had to go through the same motions as everybody else.

I ended up going to Ballard High, which was nowhere on my list of choices. Ballard had mostly white students at the time, and they were so in need of more black students to meet the city's new requirements that they were bussing kids over from the other side of town. It was in the wealthiest part of Louisville in Prospect, but I still had never heard of it. If I was pissed about being told I'd have to wait until the second semester for a chance at Doss and Central, I was mad as shit at having to start classes at Ballard!

But once I got there, I fell in love with it.

Ballard High is where I found my young self's identity. Remember, up until this point, I was a grade-A nerd. I had become a cool nerd because Derek helped me up my style and allowed me to hang out with other kids outside of school, but at Ballard is when I really started flossing. I started flossing so hard over the summer with Andrew that when school started, I didn't do any work at all!

I was still girl-crazy from the summer, and now I was seeing girls on a different side of town, so I just kept wilding out and focusing on them instead of school. Me, 'Mr. I'm-The-Number-One-Kid-In-The-City', went from one extreme of getting all A's and being a scholar, to the other extreme of getting nothing but D's and F's on my first report card. I freaked all the way out—and Derek did too! That was the first time he ever put me on punishment for bad grades, and it was the last time, too.

I got it together after that, but I still kept coming out of my shell. Through 9th grade, I started really fitting into Ballard. By the time Doss called and said they finally had a spot for me for second semester, I didn't want to leave! I'm glad I didn't transfer, because at the end of my 9th grade year is when I started playing football.

Before this, I had always been a huge basketball fan and had never actually played football in my life. I tried playing in a little league one year when I was younger, but I just didn't feel it. By the time high school came around, I had to make myself learn to love the sport of football, but that got easier when I fell out of love with basketball.

One day at a court, two guys who had been best friends for so long that they were like brothers, got into a fight over a game—and they ended up never being friends again, all over that one dumb argument about that one dumb game. I don't remember exactly what it was about, but I do remember thinking, "Wow, this is the only sport I've ever seen that can tear two brothers apart," and that made a huge impact on me.

After the type of blow-up argument me and Camp had over a game of spades, I had really admired those two guys' relationship with each other. They weren't blood-related, but they had each other's backs better than a lot of real families—but basketball was strong enough to break that. After seeing that, I didn't want anything else to do with it.

But still, when they announced over the speakers towards the end of the school year, "Everybody interested in playing football this year, meet Coach Calvin in the gym," I'd be lying if I say I went with honest intentions at first! I just went so I could get out of class on that particular day, as soon as I set foot in the gym, I knew I had to change my story, quick.

When I walked in, all I could see and hear were a whole bunch of big, loud, older boys calling out threats to every single one of us who walked in the gym.

"What y'all come out here for?"

"It better be football, I know that!"

"Anybody I see in here right now, and I don't see this summer out on the field for practice, we gon' beat y'all asses!"

I felt like I was in one of those scenes in a movie when a guard is walking a prisoner to their cell for the first time, and all the other hard prisoners are heckling them.

"Hey, you! What you come in here for?"

I wasn't sure who exactly was calling me out, but I knew what I had to say.

"I'm here for football."

When I got home, I told Derek, "Hey Dad, I'm playing football next year."

"What?"

"Yeah, yeah," I said as I put the summer practice schedule on the refrigerator. "Don't let me miss this!"

Summer finally came, and one day I was at my grandmother's house when Derek called me. "Rob, you know you got practice today."

This time it was my turn to say, "What?"

He came, picked me up, and took me out to school, and that was the beginning of my football journey. Even though I started on a whim and kind of out of fear, joining the football team turned out to be one of the best decisions in my life.

Coach Calvin made me a wide receiver, and I instantly became a part of a family. Unlike basketball, where everyone's on the same team, but you can still outshine each other, football taught me that some things really couldn't get done unless you depend on and trust others. Those two friends breaking up over an argument in basketball was still in my head, and I saw quickly that in football, everybody has each other's back no matter what. If one player is fighting or has an issue, then all other eighty-nine players are fighting and have an issue.

Even though those players were harassing us at first in the gym that day, once I joined the team, all those older players and coaches really took me under their wings and showed me the ropes. I learned that football has its own kind of system where if you work hard, be a real team player, and put your heart into it, you'll be taken care of. It was my first experience of having a big family who was consistent, especially when it came to brotherhood.

I would go weeks and months without talking to Camp, and it was starting to wear on me. Even though I missed him and wanted our companionship back, my football team made the separation from him easier. It was like I lost one brother and got eighty-nine brothers back. We would do all kinds of stuff with each other outside of practices and games, and I started to take a lot of pride in my new family. I was even more proud when I was able to start mentoring other players as I got into the swing of things.

It might have been simple to them, but it meant so much to me. Nobody at school actually knew I was in foster care, since at this point, Derek literally called me his son in front of people, and I was easily calling him my dad. It definitely wasn't something I was about to go around sharing with everybody, especially since I was finally hitting my stride. Being in foster care was embarrassing to me! And now that I was one of the top three jokesters in school, I really didn't want to give any of my football brothers material to joke about me. We were all kind of jokesters and pranksters, but I was real good at holding my own against jokes, and that was the one thing I didn't want to be made fun of. I didn't want anyone to have a reason to look at me any differently, and I didn't want to lose them.

The only person at Ballard who might have had an idea I was in foster care was our principal, Ms. Allen. As well as things were going, my social worker would have to show up from time to time, and even though she didn't make a big show of it, it was probably easy to pick up on by Ms. Allen. She never directly said anything to me about it, but she would always seem to go out of her way to do things to come through for me.

Ms. Allen was a white lady, but she didn't care if you were white, black, yellow, or purple; she was going to treat everyone the same. Everyone at Ballard loved her, teachers and students, and if you had a problem with her, then you had a problem with everybody! Every time someone tried to talk bad about her, everyone who heard it jumped to her defense. She was one of those principals who really cared about the school and her students, and she fought for us in a lot of ways. She didn't support any type of dress code, but she didn't have a problem snatching up a girl and telling her to put on some clothes. Our school excelled in academics and athletics, but unlike others, she supported both parts equally.

Just like the guys on the football team, Ms. Allen took me under her watch and looked out for me the best she could. When it came to different activities for our school, she always picked me to help host or be involved, no matter what it was. One time some of us football guys even put together a Temptations group for the halftime at the homecoming basketball game, and Ms. Allen actually rented tuxedoes for us. It was such a hit that we even performed at a few pep rallies!

She was just a good lady, and she helped me through what was about to turn into a tumultuous time in high school.

On top of joining the football team, I also met two of my best friends at Ballard, Kev, and Damon. We hung out so much; we were like the three amigos. We all ended up getting jobs working at St. Matthews mall so that just helped our friendship even more.

One day we were all working on a Sunday, but because the mall closed an hour earlier, we couldn't leave to catch the bus just yet. Most people would sit around the mall to wait, so usually, we would close our stores down and wait in the food court area.

While we were sitting there waiting, I saw these security alarm beams up under the counters of these different stores and got kind of excited because I had seen them on TV, but never in real life. I decided I was going to try out my stealth skills. So, I got on the floor, trying to crawl under the beams like I was a cat burglar or something. I was creeping under these laser beams when I looked up and saw two legs standing right behind my head.

I stopped and turned around to get a better look at who was behind me when I heard, "Get up, nigger."

It was the lady security officer whom me and my friends had seen in the mall all the time, along with the younger guy security officer. She was the supervisor, so we just looked at her and said, "Ma'am, you're not supposed to talk to us like that."

"I can talk to y'all any kind of way I want," she responded. "Like I said, get off the floor, nigger."

Kev, Damon, and I were in shock, but she asked us what we were still doing there, so we told her that we were workers waiting on our bus to come. We kept trying to tell her that she shouldn't have been talking to us that way, but instead of listening, she went a step further and kicked us out of the mall.

The next weekend we all tried to come to work, but we found out they had banned all three of us from entering into the mall!

It turned out that the security office had sent letters to all three stores that we worked at, telling them that we were banned from the mall altogether. We had essentially gotten wrongfully fired, so we wound up calling Kev's mom, Ms. Jackie, and she helped us set up a meeting with the owner of the mall.

The owner pulled all of us into his office to figure out what was going on because we had never caused any issues or had any complaints. However, the security officer was saying something completely different. So we told our side of the story, but the lady security officer made up this huge lie about how we were disrespectful, cussing her out, and she never called us any names!

Things almost went wrong because, as far as character witnesses went, we didn't really have any. Ms. Jackie knew who Damon and I were, but she didn't know us enough to say that we weren't troublemakers, so she was kind of in the same boat as the owner: trying to figure out whose word was the truth.

The younger security officer was in the office with us too, but he didn't say a word the whole time. The only thing he said when asked was that she was telling the truth, but he said it so unconvincingly that the owner knew the lady was lying. For Ms. Jackie's part, she figured out the lady was lying when she kept accusing us of cussing her out.

Ms. Jackie asked the lady, "Well, who was cussing at you?"

The lady switched her story up again, "It wasn't all of them; it was just one of them."

"OK, so which one was it?"

The lady pointed at Kev, and that blew any chance she had of trying to lie on us. Kev was a church kid, and out of all three of us, he didn't cuss, ever!

We finally left the meeting, and by the time we did, both the owner and Ms. Jackie knew for a fact that the lady was a liar. When it was all finished, the mall owner told us we weren't banned anymore, and all three of us got our jobs back. Experiencing stuff like this together brought me, Kev, and Damon closer as friends, and it's lasted even up to this day.

Damon worked a lot more than Kev and I did, so while we were all tight, I spent a lot of time at Kev's house when I could. Derek usually never minded, and one particular weekend, our school was out for a holiday, so I had spent the night at Kev's house for the whole weekend. Kev and his brothers wanted me to stay, so I called Derek up to ask him if I could spend an extra night.

Derek said I had been gone for a while already, and he wanted me to come home, so I said alright and got my stuff together. I was upset about it because I knew all I was going to do when I got home was just sit there and do nothing, but I also knew there was nothing else I could say about it.

So, Derek pulled up in his droptop Mustang with my younger foster brother in the front seat, and I got in.

Now, it's worth saying that around this time, I was still

a pretty good kid. I was making good grades, I was on the football team, I was working a weekend job, and I occasionally spent the night at my friend's house. I didn't give Derek any trouble anywhere near what my other foster brothers were doing.

I was sitting in the middle of the backseat, and Derek could see the sad look on my face.

Derek asked me, "What's wrong with you back there?"

"Nothing," I replied.

"What, you mad 'cause you can't spend the night?"

"Well, you told me to come home, so I gotta come home."

I didn't say anything else, so Derek started driving off. We weren't too far from Kev's house when Derek looked back at me again and saw that I still looked upset.

"You need to fix your face!" And with that, he reached back and punched me in my legs.

I couldn't believe it, and said, "Dad, why are you hitting me?"

He stopped the car and was trying to reach around to grab me, but he had his seatbelt on and couldn't quite get to me. Before things could get worse, I jumped out of the car and took off running down the street. We were on a one-way street, so he couldn't just turn around to get me, so I kept running down more one-way streets to keep him from catching up to me.

I finally got back to Kev's house, and both Kev and his mom were sitting on the front porch. When they saw me coming, they asked me what I was doing, but right as I got there, Derek pulled up and called out, "Rob, get your ass in this car!"

Still pissed off, I yelled back, "Nah, man, what the fuck are you hitting me for?"

Derek had never done anything like that to me, and as I said, I wasn't a kid who was getting in trouble, so I didn't think there was a reason for him to put his hands on me at all. I was refusing to get in the car, and it took Kev's mom to calm me down, and then tell me I couldn't spend the night anyway, so I needed to get in the car. I ended up getting in the car and going home, and he put me on punishment.

To Kev and Ms. Jackie, I was just a disrespectful kid running away and cussing out his dad in front of people. Kev didn't know me at the time, and so he thought I was some unruly kid with no type of home training. They just assumed Derek was my biological dad, and it wasn't until some years later when I told them about my life in foster care and everything else, that they understood why I was so upset with Derek that day.

So not knowing my situation, on top of the fact that I didn't go to church much, seeing that kind of helped Kev get this idea that he was a little better than me, which I found to be funny!

Even though he didn't understand me all the way, we were still tight, even in class at school. Kev and I both had a biology class with one of our favorite teachers, Mr. Tuck, and we would compete with each other all year, trying to be the best at our tests and assignments.

At the end of our 10th grade year, Mr. Tuck told us, "I'm tired of y'all always competing for the high scores on tests and everything, so what we're gonna do is have Rob versus Kev. If you think Kev's gonna win, get on his side. If you think Rob's gonna win, get on his side of the classroom."

All our classmates split up on either side of the room, and Mr. Tuck pulled out all the material for the whole year and asked us question after question. Whichever one of us answered the most questions right was going to be considered the smartest and king of the class.

We got down to the last five minutes in class, and Kev and I were tied. Everybody in class was hyped up, "We gotta break the tie! We gotta break it!"

So Mr. Tuck decided that we could both ask each other a question about anything, and Kev asked him, "Does it have to be about biology?"

"No, it can be any subject, anything."

I went first, and I asked him a question that he got wrong. So now it was Kev's turn to ask me a question, and the pressure was on. If I got it right, I would be crowned the king, but if I got it wrong, we would have to go back and forth asking questions until one of us was right.

Kev was a churchgoing kid, so he said, "Name me five books in the Bible." He assumed I was some type of heathen and that there was no way possible I would know anything about the Bible!

I asked him, "Are you talking about New Testament or Old Testament?"

He got this smirk on his face and said, "Old Testament," as if the New Testament would be too easy. Then he took it a step further just to be cocky, waving his hand at me, "Don't even name me five, just name me three."

"OK, so three books in the Bible, Old Testament?"

"Yep."

What he didn't know about me was that I used to sing in the boys' choir and go to church, and we would always warm up with a particular song about all the books in the Bible.

So when Kev asked me that question, I started baiting him with my answer. "Was Genesis one?" I asked uncertainly.

"OK, you got one, OK. Two more, two more."

I tried to bait him up a little bit more with my next answer, "Uh, is Exodus one?" But I couldn't hold back too much longer, and before he could respond, I decided to go ahead and get him. "Genesis, Exodus, Leviticus, Numbers, Deuteronomy, Joshua, Judges, Ruth, 1st Samuel, 2nd Samuel..."

As I named all the books in order, the whole class went wild! I went out with a big bang, Kev felt bad for being so cocky, and I was crowned king of the class. Kev and I are still best friends to this day, but every now and then, I still have to remind him who the king is!

There were some arguments and misunderstandings here and there, but overall, life felt pretty good. I had lost touch with my older brother, but I had made friends who were like brothers, on top of having a huge football family.

The same was true when it came to Derek. During my 10th grade year, even though there were a few small disagreements, my relationship with Derek had been getting stronger and stronger. We were so solid that nobody could tell we weren't related already, so when he started focusing on legally adopting me as his son, I was beyond happy! It seemed only right to make it official.

We started the process, and a day came when we were at the lawyer's office, pretty much about to finish all the paperwork of me becoming Derek's son. The whole meeting went great, but right before we walked out, the lawyer asked, "Hey, so what's his name gonna be?"

When the lawyer asked that, I said one name, and Derek said another. The only difference in our answers was my middle name, but the lawyer just laughed it off, "Hey, I guess y'all got something to talk about now!"

We left the office and got in the car, but Derek was mad, telling me how I embarrassed him in there.

"You really disrespected me in there today."

I couldn't understand how or why, at all! We had always talked about me changing my last name to Bowman, but we had never said anything about me taking on his middle name.

I tried to explain to him, "Dad, I wasn't trying to embarrass you, but we talked about this before. I don't mind taking your last name, but I want to keep as much of the name that my mom gave me as possible."

I was sixteen years old and had adjusted well to a

different life, but that didn't mean I didn't love my mom, or I wanted to erase any part of her memory in my life.

Derek was the type that when he got mad, he would do childish things like give you the silent treatment. He never really had gotten upset with me before, but for the first time, he ignored me for almost three to four days straight. Being a kid, I didn't think too much of it. I just ignored him right back. We would walk right by each other in the house like neither one of us existed.

As I mentioned before, Derek had other foster kids in the home, but a lot of them just assumed because of how close we were that I was his actual son. Some knew I was a foster kid too, but it was kind of understood by the way he treated me that I wasn't going anywhere, whereas in their case, they would eventually have to leave. So, when the other kids would get in trouble, Derek would punish them in a different way by taking their house key away so they couldn't just come and go as they please.

But one day, Derek took my house key away. He had never done that to me before, so when he did, I started to think, *OK, now you're not treating me like your son anymore, you're treating me like a regular foster kid. Cool.*

So now, all that summer, I had to work with the other kids to coordinate my schedule to make sure I wouldn't be locked out. Derek let it go on for a couple more days, but I didn't say a word about it. That just made him even more enraged.

One day over the summer going into my junior year, I was sitting downstairs eating cereal, and Derek was standing across the way in the kitchen, ironing his clothes for work. I don't remember his exact words, but he said something to tease me about taking my key away. Instead of snapping back, since I couldn't do anything about it anyway, all I said was, "Whatever you wanna do, it doesn't matter to me."

That must have been too much for him to take because he walked over and smacked the bowl of cereal off the table, and all the milk and cereal spilled all over me. He got in my face and said, "You know what? Take your butt upstairs. You gonna get the fuck out of my house."

I couldn't believe it, and said, "Wow, so now you're kicking me out?"

"I'm calling your fucking social worker, and you getting the fuck outta here!"

I was in complete disbelief. All we had been doing was not speaking, and now he was ready to kick me out because I wasn't talking back or disrespecting him? Crazy.

So I go upstairs and start packing my stuff, and the whole time Derek is walking back and forth, going in and out of my room, just going off on me and cussing me out. "You ungrateful, you gon' realize!" I still wasn't saying much of anything to him, just packing, and finally, he started going for my aquarium.

Anybody who knew me knew that I loved fish, and I had saved my money up and bought my own aquarium. It was my personal project, and I loved it. Whenever I wanted to chill, I would turn the lights off in my room, put on some Sade, and just watch my fish. That was my thing.

Derek knew it, so he came in my room, reaching for it and yelled, "I'll dump this thing on the ground!"

All I said was, "It's your house, if you want twenty gallons of water on your floor, go ahead." I loved my fish, but in the end, I just felt like, what could I really do? He said he was kicking me out, and it was his house anyway. I was crying and upset, but what could I argue with him for?

I guess that wasn't the reaction he wanted, so he left my aquarium alone and stormed out of my room. He came back in my room one last time, but this time he had the last pictures I had of my mom and the newspaper clippings of my mom's death that was in the paper.

Starting from the top, Derek starts ripping the pictures and the newspapers, gloating in my face, "You see this shit?"

I don't know what came over me, but at that moment, all I knew was this was not my father. What type of person would take the last memories of someone's mom and just rip it up in their face, all because of a little disagreement?

My social worker finally came to get me and took me to a home with a lot of other foster boys down by Shawnee Park, which was a neighborhood that was closer to where Camp was living. It was a rough neighborhood, over in the West End of Louisville, where people got shot faithfully every weekend. The change was a huge shock after living with Derek for almost two years, but after what he had done, I knew I didn't want to go back.

Derek came over a couple of times after that incident

to where I was living to try to get me to come home, but I just couldn't. Things were insanely bad at this new home, but after Derek showed how selfish and uncaring he could be by destroying the last pictures I had of my mom, I knew I'd rather struggle than to ever live with him again. He even tried to bring some of my foster brothers to try to convince me, but I never looked at him the same again.

5

NEVER LOOK BACK

At sixteen years old and starting my junior year of high school, I found myself back in a precarious situation. Even though I'd been in steady foster care for some years now, this was the first time in a while where things really felt hopeless.

Having lived with Derek for almost two years, I was used to having my own space and not having to worry about much of anything: I had food, I had an allowance, and I had security. But after Derek flipped and kicked me out, my social worker put me in a home with a foster mom that was the furthest thing from having my own room with an aquarium.

There were way too many of us in that small house, but I had hope when I realized my new foster mom was one of my mom's old friends. I was in my room when I heard a woman calling out, "Where's the new kid?" All the other foster kids started calling for me, and when I finally came out to the front room, I heard that same woman gasp, "Oh my God, Mone?" The only people who ever called me Mone were the ones who knew me back when I lived with Herman in Cotter Homes, but I still didn't recognize her.

"You know me?"

"Yeah, I know you, you Donna's son!"

It turned out she was one of my mom's friends from back in the day, and I was too excited! Finally, after so long, I had met someone who knew who I was and where I came from, and I thought, *You know what? This might turn out nice.*

That hope was short-lived though, because our foster mom didn't even live there with us. She would come by just once a month to drop off groceries that would barely last a week, and that was it. It was a constant battle even to keep those groceries alive because the house had roaches so bad, they literally would swarm the food inside of the refrigerator! When you went to lay down, roaches would come swarming out of the mattress and had no issues crawling over your stomach.

The house was filthy, but she would keep her pretend boyfriend there just so that if a social worker happened to stop by, there would be an "adult" in the house. But he was always on drugs and wouldn't even be around much, so me and the other foster boys were pretty much on our own. Without any adult there, that meant a lot of the times the boys wouldn't even go to school. Some of them had failed school a couple of times, so they were all in 5th grade and lower but were older. They would just do whatever they wanted, and I felt like as the oldest kid there, maybe I should have been doing something to help keep them in school. They all looked up to me, but a sixteen-year-old kid wasn't enough to run a whole household of kids. I was barely keeping things together for myself.

Even though I was further out of the way, my principal, Ms. Allen, kept looking out for me. I had to walk a few blocks every day, but she made sure a bus would still come to pick me up for school. I kept playing football, too, and nobody knew how bad things had gotten for me at home. To try to get some money in my pocket, I started working at Great Steak and Potatoes, but because I was doing so much in school and I lived way over in Shawnee Park, I could only work on the weekends. So, I wasn't making a whole bunch of money that would help me out through the week, but it was better than having nothing.

After shifts, I was able to take food home from my job, and I would try my hardest to bring as much as I could, but all the food we could get in the house would only have a shelf life of about two or three days before the roaches in the fridge got to it. That meant, for the most part, every week for at least half of the week, we had nothing to eat at all. At this point, I was literally going to school so that I could eat. I was starving all the time, and it changed the way I viewed life.

One of the only good things about living in Shawnee Park was that it was close to my best friend Kev's house. I spent as much time at his house as I could to escape the terrible reality that my life had become, and one day I was over there hanging out, starving out of my mind. Like I mentioned earlier, nobody really knew what was going on with me outside of when they saw me at school, so my friend Kev just thought I had gotten into it with my dad (Derek) and was now living with one of my aunts. Even if it meant I might get help, I was just too embarrassed to tell anyone.

So we were hanging out, and Kev was eating a bowl a cereal. It felt like I'd been wandering around a desert for years, and I'd finally stumbled on another person splashing around in a river, but I was too scared to ask if I could come over there. Sitting there trying to play it cool, I was watching Kev like a hawk as he finished his cereal when I noticed something crazy. He left his milk in the bowl!

Is he about to dump it out? I thought.

Having no idea what was running through my mind, Kev stood up to take his bowl full of milk in the kitchen, but before he could get too far, I blurted out, "Hey man, what are you about to do with that milk?"

"Oh, I'm just about to dump it out."

As casually as I could, I said, "Man, let me drink it."

He stopped and looked at me like I was crazy. "What?"

"Yeah," I said, "let me drink the milk, don't waste it."

Kev looked like he couldn't believe we were even having this conversation. "Rob, man, just fix you some cereal."

"Oh, is...is that OK?" I was so desperate for food, even being offered some seemed unreal.

"Rob, dude, go fix some cereal."

It was probably such a small thing to him, but Kev had no idea how big it was for me to be able to fix a bowl of cereal at his house. On the outside looking in, everything about me looked fine, but every day I was barely making it.

During this time, Derek had come back around a few times to try to get me to move back in with him, but even though I was getting by every day, I would have rather lived in the struggle I was in than to go back with him. He brought some of my other foster brothers with him on different occasions to see if they could convince me, but there was nothing any of them could say to me to replace the memory I had of Derek tearing up my mom's pictures in my face.

Things kept going rough like this at the foster home until eventually the school the younger foster boys were supposed to be attending started noticing their absences more. They missed school for weeks at a time, so when the school got involved, the state got involved. The home was closed down, and in the middle of my junior year, I was placed into another foster home with the Barbours.

The Barbours lived out on Goldsmith Lane close to Bashford Manor Mall, and they were a nice family: they had their own little girl, they gave me my own room, the house was clean, and they definitely didn't do any of the crazy stuff my previous foster mom had done when it came to food. When I moved in with them, I had officially moved out of the school district, but my principal still kept sending the bus to get me—things kind of settled down through to my senior year. There were only four interests I had on my mind at that time: sports, school, work, and girls. I didn't cause any trouble, and I didn't want any trouble. I just wanted a peaceful, stable place to live!

By this time, I had gotten a girlfriend, Tasha Wilson. I had been trying to get with her for years, so we started spending a lot of time together at her house. I didn't have a curfew, and even though I was living pretty well with the Barbours, every time I was over at the Wilsons' house, it was like taking another breath of fresh air. The Wilsons weren't rich or anything, but Tasha's family was middle class, and they just had so much. There was a pool table downstairs, and her dad had this amazing pond in their backyard. I loved going over there just to be around them. When I was with them, it made me look at things differently and helped me aspire to have better in my own life.

During this time, going from the end of my junior year to the summer, I ended up losing Kev as a friend for a while. He had gotten saved at his church and had to go on a "sabbatical," and I guess I didn't fit the right category for good influences! He wasn't allowed to hang with me anymore, and I was pretty mad because we had planned out prom outfits, dates, and everything...but he couldn't even go!

Even though I was missing my best friend, one of our other football friends, Ron, started hanging out with me. He was a year younger than me, but we got real cool with each other and even worked a job together shredding paper. To this day, we're still tight.

So at the Barbours' house, I was still playing football and now track, but even though now I had a more stable family, I still didn't have any real guidance when it came to my future. Coach Calvin was my football and my track coach, and one day he came to me and told me Bowling Green University wanted to talk to me about a scholarship.

I was so young-minded and dumb that the only Bowling Green I had ever heard about was Bowling Green, Kentucky, where the University of Western Kentucky was. *Man,* I thought, *they must be a small school.* I had already done my test to go to school for CAD, architecture, and drafting and was set on going to Louisville Tech for it. Even though I had been doing football and track, I wasn't so in love with either of them to the point where I was to the point where I wanted to go to school just for sports. Plus, I had been kicking ass in track, and I thought I was too good to be running for some small school!

So, I basically shut down the whole conversation when Coach Calvin came to me about Bowling Green.

The thing about it is, my coach knew about my situation with foster care like Ms. Allen, and I wish he would've taken more of a leadership role in my life by making me talk to the school and find out about the opportunity to see whether I wanted it or not. He did with some students, but not all, and definitely not with me. I really could have used his guidance at this critical point in my life.

It wasn't until a year later after I graduated high school when me and Kev were playing a football video game that I figured out the Bowling Green University Coach Calvin was talking about was actually the huge school up in Ohio! I wound up going to one of the high school football games with Kev because his brothers were still playing, and I pulled Coach Calvin to the side.

"Hey coach, were you talking about Bowling Green University, the one in Ohio?"

"Oh, yeah."

"Why didn't you tell me?"

"Well, you were the one saying you didn't wanna talk to them!"

"Yeah, 'cause I was thinking you were talking about some small school in Kentucky!"

I had turned down a possible scholarship from that university without even talking to them, just being young and dumb, but more than that completely left without any guidance.

In our senior year right before graduation, I got my girlfriend got pregnant. We were both scared out of our minds...but we didn't want to tell anybody! We knew we were just about free from high school, but we still were worried about what to do. All the clichés and struggles about teenage pregnancy were hanging over our heads, and none of it spelled out an easy path for us.

One day while I was out playing basketball, Tasha had a miscarriage. Everything happened so fast, and so unexpectedly, I wasn't able to be there for her when it happened. The loss put a severe strain on our relationship, and we both dealt with it the best way we knew how as teenagers who were keeping it a secret. My girlfriend made me feel guilty for not being there, and to compensate, I spent every free second I had with her outside of school, work, and football.

We graduated from high school, and now I was going to Louisville Tech. Still living with the Barbours, it was literally a fifteen-minute walk right down the street from their house, and I was killing it! In my first semester, I had made it on the dean's list for my program, and everything was good...until my social worker called me one day when I was at my girlfriend's house.

"Hey, they don't want you to come back."

What?

Tasha and I had stayed together through the miscarriage and graduation, and because of all the trauma, I was spending almost all of my free time with Tasha now. I guess it started to look really suspect to Mr. and Mrs. Barbour. Like I said earlier, I didn't have a curfew or anything when I lived with them, so for an eighteen-year-old college kid, it was a license to freedom.

If I wanted to stay out until 3 a.m. with my girlfriend, I did! It wasn't like I was running the streets, doing drugs, or anything like that, and the Barbours on their part didn't actually say anything directly to me. But they did start forming their own assumptions of what was going on and took some action.

I was shocked and confused, and once again, I thought, *What did I do?* Unfortunately, I wouldn't find out until twenty years later in life from Mrs. Barbour that they didn't think I was on drugs, they just had a problem with me staying out so late all of the time. They never said anything to me about it, which is why I couldn't understand why it was an issue. But they figured that if Mr. Barbour wasn't staying out late, then why was I?

I can't say I understood their reasons behind it all, but it was what it was.

Since I was eighteen, my social worker couldn't place me in another home, but there was a shelter downtown on the east end side of Louisville that they could put me in, and that's where I ended up. Unlike being in a foster home, the shelter was designed for getting people out of the shelter and into their own place to stay, so during the day, no one could just kind of hang around. Everyone had to be out either working or looking for work until the evening and once you started working, they would take half of your check to save for you and give you the other half to live off of.

The other significant change was my school was now on the other side of town. So now, I was still in college, but I had to make sure I made it there every day while also focusing on working. When I lived with the Barbours, I was able to walk to school. But at the shelter, I had to take the public bus three hours ahead of my first class starting, just to make sure I got there on time.

I would get there so early, one of the ladies who worked at the school saw me and asked if I wanted to open the bookstore since I was there at 6:30 a.m. My first class started at 9 a.m., so I picked that job up easily. I would then go to my classes, and after school, I picked up another job, Monday through Thursday at Gattyland, kind of like a Chuck E. Cheese type of place. My last class ended at 2 p.m. so I would work at Gattyland from 4 p.m. - 9 p.m.

On Friday, I didn't have any classes, so I worked at Gattyland during the day, and I picked up yet another job at Krispy Kreme, working the third shift Friday through Sunday, working twelve-hour shifts.

So at this point, I was trying to manage working three jobs and going to school, and it just started wearing me down. For months, I was exhausted all the time. The tipping point came when I hurt my back at Krispy Kreme. Now, I was trying to manage this schedule with an injury, but the pain from my back started taking a toll on me.

During this time, I was still dating Tasha, and her mom knew I was staying in the shelter. She told me, "Rob, I asked Tasha when you first started being put in the shelter did she want you to live with us, but Tasha told me no." I get it now that Tasha was still angry with me from miscarrying, but she basically left me in the shelter.

At the same time, Kev's mom, Ms. Jackie, had asked him if he wanted me to live with them. But Kev's older brother had just moved out to go to college, and it was his first time having his own room. He didn't want to give up having his own space, so he told his mom no, too.

Also, Kev didn't know everything about me then when it came to foster care and what all I was going through, and he had seen me get into it with Derek in front of his house. In his mind, he had watched me cuss out my dad, so he was thinking, "Man, what kind of dude is this that cusses his parent out?" But he didn't realize everything that was going on behind the scenes back then.

But still, the two most influential people in my life at the time, my girlfriend and my best friend, left me in a shit situation.

I finally gave out under the pressure: I quit all my jobs and started thinking about how I could get out of the shelter. I couldn't handle it anymore. Sleep was nonexistent to me, and it felt like I was being slowly consumed down to nothing.

My grandmother still lived in the city on Grand Avenue, so I called her and asked if I could move in with her for a bit. She had always had someone living with her over the years, like my uncles or cousins, but no one was there now, so she said yes. I moved in and stayed with her for a little under a year, but now I was even further away from the college, so it gave me a reason to drop out.

I started working at the Curio Journal, one of our local newspapers. Eventually, I lost that job, and I moved out of my grandmother's house to live with one of my friends from high school, Damon.

He had his own apartment in the projects, so I just stayed with him sleeping on his floor for a couple of months. Damon was smoking weed back then, but I was able to get us both jobs at a place called Airborne Express, and we started making the most money we had ever made at that point, almost $800 a week with overtime.

I was used to bringing in weekly checks around $200 up until this point, so I felt like I was ballin'! Getting paid for four weeks of work after one week was blowing my mind. On top of the pay, it was a super easy job, so moving out into my own place was starting to become more and more of a reality.

Working at Airborne Express, I was close to the airport near a small town where the Bethels, my old foster family, still lived. I really wanted to see how they were doing, so one day on my lunch break, I drove over to their house just to talk to them, and I was shocked to see that they were amazed at whom I had grown up to be as a young man.

By now, people who knew us had heard stories about Camp and the path he was taking. I guess it was a shock to people to learn about the directions we had taken.

When we were younger, Camp was the one who had shown a lot of promise and talent. I had always been coined as having an "attitude." On top of that, I was the darker-skinned, kind of nappy-headed one, while he was more fair-skinned and had good hair, so people had assumed that I was going to be this thug or nobody in life, while Camp was going to be the successful one.

But when we got split up after leaving Uncle Omar and Aunt Jackie, and he was placed with Derek's mom, Camp started hanging with the wrong crowd in her neighborhood and just went in a completely different direction. So now here I was, standing in front of the Bethels and all they kept saying was, "Wow, this is Robert! Oh my God, you're just doing so well!"

It just made me think, again, *man, what type of kid was I?* In my mind, I didn't do anything that bad!

In any case, our stint at Airborne Express was short-lived because we were using Damon's car to get to work, but somebody stole it. We couldn't make it into work one day...well, truth be told, we were trying to get into something that day and avoid going into work, past his car being stolen! But still, his mom never called in for us so we could be covered, and we wound up getting fired.

Now, I am sitting here jobless in the projects with my friend, looking back on everything that's happened in my life over the last year, and I just realize: this is not the life I want. This is just not it.

So, me and Damon start talking about selling drugs, and our conversations are getting serious. Before we could get into it, I reminded myself of the way my mom died and promised myself that I wouldn't sell drugs. Things didn't get better between Damon and me, so after we got into it one day, I stopped staying with him.

I started bouncing between some girls' houses, staying here and there for weeks and days at a time before I finally just got fed up with life.

One night I found myself at McDonald's on 2nd and Broadway, and I was so desperate and determined for a change that I walked from there, all the way to my best friend Kev's house near Chickasaw Park, which was forty blocks away. I knocked on his door and asked him, "Hey, can you take me to a military recruiter in the morning?"

Kev had already joined the military right out of high school, and now he was in the Reserves, so I knew he would help me out. He was staying with his brother JR at the time, so I asked him if I could stay there that night, and he said it was cool. So I stayed there overnight, and the next morning Kev took me to the recruiter and got everything set up so I could do my ASVAB and all the other military testing.

It was around Thanksgiving, and I told the recruiter I was trying to get out of Louisville as soon as possible. He told me the earliest he could get me out was December 28th, and that was fine with me.

Now I had a new purpose, and I was starting to feel the most confident about my life than I had in a long time. Before I left Louisville, Rosie, Kev's girlfriend, found out what I was about to do, and she invited us over to stay at her place to give me a going-away dinner. She shared an apartment with two of her friends, and they cooked a huge spaghetti dinner. We just had a great night hanging out together, and that was the last memory I made before leaving the next day.

For the first time in my life, I flew on a plane to leave Louisville for basic training on December 28th, and I never looked back. I was scared, but I was determined to change and make a better life than what I had so far.

6

SPIRIT

The day finally came when I took off in a plane to leave Louisville for the first time and touched down in Missouri to go to Fort Leonard Wood for basic training. Those nine weeks taught me a lot about myself, and I learned even more about the world that I hadn't experienced yet. Before this, I was just a country boy from a country town, and in basic, I met people from places I'd never even thought about going to. People were from New York, California, Florida, everywhere, and it was just mind-opening for me.

Now when I got there, there had been a raging snowstorm going on. The base was almost completely frozen over, so the first three days seemed perfect to me. I was calling my friend Kev reveling in it all, "Man, I should've joined the Army when you did! I can see myself doing this for the next twenty years; it's so easy!" They were telling us all these great things about the Army: how we could

retire out and be set for life, how much money we were
going to make in a month—more than I ever had—it all
sounded like nothing I'd ever heard before. I just knew it
was going to be the easiest money I'd ever made in my life.

I had no idea how much of a rude awakening I was
in for.

The next day, we finally met our drill sergeants for the
first time, and it was an experience, to say the least. See, in
the first three days of us being on the base, I thought the
people who had been talking to us so nicely *were* the drill
sergeants; I had no idea that the actual process of basic
training was delayed because of the snowstorm!

So, they put us all in a gym, and this group of sergeants
that we haven't met until now comes tearing in, yelling,
and screaming at us recruits who are now all in shock.
Everybody has their bags that they brought with them, but
on top of that, we now also have all of the military gear and
equipment that we'd been given in the previous few days.
The drill sergeants get right to smoking us, screaming at all
of us to hold our belongings high and not to let anything
touch the ground. In that moment, I couldn't have been
happier that I had listened to Kev before when he warned
me, "Don't pack a bunch of stuff, just bring a little
backpack."

As I looked around, I saw some people who had whole
suitcases, and the sergeants were wearing them out.

"Oh, so you must think you at Palm Springs!
OK, OK..."

I was so glad all I had was my little backpack!

They smoked us for about forty more minutes or so before they finally took us to another room where we met our personal drill sergeants, the ones who would be responsible for us during basic. I had two: a man and a woman. They introduced who they were, the name of the platoon I would be a part of, and they explained how they were going to help guide us through the next nine weeks. They were talking to us in normal voices, and everything felt great at this point, but our minds were still all over the place in shock from what had just happened.

After this, it was time to eat, so we all got in a line and marched to go to the chow hall, and when we get there, the sergeants are screaming again! So now we're all sitting down eating, and they're just giving us hell.

"What are you doing?"

"You're just in here to eat, quit looking around!"

"What are you looking around for?"

It's chaos all over the place, and all anyone is trying to do is just keep their head down and eat without getting called out or picked on. So I'm still sitting at the table and eating, trying to figure out how fast I can get out of this room with the drill sergeants where pandemonium has broken out, to outside, where it might be a little better because there are not as many sergeants out there yet.

I see a trash can literally four feet away from me, so I make my getaway plan: hurry up and finish eating, get up, throw my tray away, then hightail it for the door. It seems simple enough and foolproof, so I stand up and turn around when BOOM...I'm face to face with a drill sergeant.

At 6'4", I'm taller than just about everybody I meet, and this drill sergeant was no different. He was about 5'9", so he was staring up at me from under his brimmed hat while my tray was still in my hand, and we're just standing there staring each other down like we're in a duel in one of those old Western movies.

It's important to know that since it had only been a few days and the base's operations were slowed down by the snowstorm, we had gone through a condensed version of what's called replacement. Replacement is the process when you first arrive on base where they not only give you your military gear and equipment, but they also teach you about the military customs and different things like that. This usually is supposed to take between seven to ten days, but since the base had been frozen over, they crammed our replacement into only three days! Needless to say, the meaning of some of it was missed just because of how fast the whole learning process went. I kept hearing specific phrases over and over, but still didn't know what they meant!

There was one particular phrase I heard that I thought meant "excuse me," because every time somebody walked in, we would always say, "At ease!"

The drill sergeant is still standing there in front of me, so I do the polite thing and say excuse me, military-style, "At ease, drill sergeant."

He looks at me with a blank look on his face. "What you say?"

In my mind, I've already said excuse me to him once, so I'm convinced that he's just trying to pick on me. All the other sergeants are still in the room screaming at people, and somehow out of everybody, I've gotten this one's attention. *Alright, Rob, you said excuse me once, just say it again. No big deal.*

So, I repeat myself, "At ease, drill sergeant."

He repeats himself, too. "What did you say?"

Now I know for sure that he's picking on me because I've said excuse me twice, and he's still giving me a hard time, just to be mean!

Again, I tell myself, *OK Rob, say excuse me one more time.* This time, though, I'm a little more uncertain.

"At ease, drill sergeant...?"

At this point, I just don't get it. I've said excuse me three times, and here this guy is giving me a hard time for no reason. He's black, I'm black, and with the type of mindset I had been "fresh off the block" from Louisville, I just felt like I was being set up for no reason. I had never been in or around the military, and I had never known anybody personally who was in the military growing up. This was all completely brand new to me, and I had no type of idea of how things were supposed to go or how I was supposed to act.

This time he tells me to sit down, and my frustration finally boils over. I throw my tray on the table, slam back down in my seat, and fold my arms across my chest. "Man!" I huff.

That was all it took.

The drill sergeant immediately hollers out, "HEY! Hey everybody! I got one. I got one!"

As soon as he yells, all these drill sergeants start weaving through the tables to get to me like sharks coming to feast, and as soon as they surround me, they start.

"GET UP, PRIVATE, GET UP!"

I stand up.

"PUT YOUR HANDS BEHIND YOUR BACK, AT PARADE REST!"

Words and spit are flying from their mouths, and one particular guy is hollering at me, "Oh, Private Harris, Private Harris, I'ma have your ass in jail, you gon' be in jail! I promise you! You think you tough?"

Looking back, it was probably funny to watch: there's about six or seven people around me, and I'm taller than all of them so I have to look down to see them, but they're steady screaming out, "Don't be looking at me, soldier! DON'T BE LOOKING AT ME!"

So now I'm standing there with tears streaming down my face, trying to find something to look at past their faces, and I can hear that same sergeant who was saying he was going to put me in jail above all the others saying, "OOH, whose solider is this, I want him! Somebody, please trade me! Trade me! I wanna switch him!"

He gets right back in my face and threatens me again, "'Cause I'ma have your ass in jail. You think you tough?"

All I can think is, *what the fuck?*

Then all of a sudden, this little short guy comes out of nowhere and makes them all go away. I didn't know any ranks or anything, but later I found out he was a first sergeant, which meant he was the supervisor over all of our drill sergeants. He pulls me to the side and gives me a little advice.

"You know, Private Harris, I've seen a lot of guys come through here thinking they're tough, or that they're this or that...and they wind up in jail, or they wind up kicked out of the military..."

I'm trying to listen to him through the tears that just won't stop coming, but all I can think is, *great, now I'm being labeled a troublemaker.* Literally, all I was trying to do was get up, throw my tray away, and go outside...but nope, now I'm about to go to jail!

At this moment, I came to two conclusions: the military was not for me like I thought it was, and I was ready to go home.

He tells me to throw my tray away and go outside finally, but when I get there, there's another group of drill sergeants waiting on us and screaming, "GET ON THE GROUND! GET ON THE GROUND!!!"

Everyone's in the pushup position, and as I drop to the ground, my forearms are entirely covered in snow up to my elbows, and I'm doing my best to keep the snow from getting in my face as I hold my position. Before another thought about quitting can come in my mind, I'm trying to encourage myself, *Rob, you wanna change your life, you don't wanna sell drugs, you left to better yourself, you always promised yourself that you would do something positive for your mom...*

But it's still not enough. I want to leave.

Right at this moment, I hear somebody saying, "Hey. So everybody, if y'all wanna leave, y'all can just get up and get in this line over here because all of these people said the military is not for them, and we're gonna send them home tonight. They're gonna be home eating mama's supper and sleeping in their beds again!"

I see some people getting up, and it's hard to see what all is happening because we're still down in pushup position, but I can hear other recruits yelling, "No, don't go, don't go!"

In my peripheral vision, I can hear a guy talking to himself, saying "No, no, no, no, no!" over and over. He's trying to convince himself not to get up, but I swear even though his body stayed on the ground, I saw his spirit lift out of his body and float past me to the line. To this day, I can't believe what I saw, but if anything can make a person's spirit leave their body, what we were experiencing that day in basic training was it!

Not even seconds later, the sergeants all yell at us to get up and get in line. We do as we're told, and then we start marching. As we're going, the sergeants are taunting us, "Hey, see? Y'all not smart like them, y'all should've got over here in this line, y'all could be going home! But y'all don't wanna go home, so y'all go on and go."

So, we march on and have to walk past the people who

have gotten in that line and think they're going home. But what none of us knew was that the drill sergeants were trying to weed out who was weak. I was so close to giving up and getting in that line, but one last thought saved me, *What's there for me to go back to Louisville for? Selling drugs?*

It was tough, but I knew no matter what, I didn't want to do that. So, I kept marching.

No sooner did I have that short conversation with myself, then I heard all the drill sergeants start ripping into those kids in that line.

"GET BACK DOWN!"

They smoked them even longer as we marched off, and all I could think was, *Wow, I'm so glad I didn't go over there.*

That was my introduction to my time in the Army, but really it was the beginning of me growing up from a boy to man. The military made me realize the abilities I possessed as a person that probably would have gone unnoticed for a long time if I had never joined. My drill sergeants saw things in me that I didn't see, and immediately they made me the platoon guide over our platoon, which was my first leadership position in the Army.

It was a little shocking to realize what I had in me, especially as I was now partially in charge of all these different people from different places. I learned quickly that the perceptions I'd gotten of people and their cities from TV weren't always right: everybody from New York wasn't a thug! No matter where people came from and their personalities, everybody was human.

As I realized that, it became easier to stand in the role of not just a leader, but a mentor. On the inside, I still felt like a little kid who had a lot to learn, but I didn't really have a choice. At eighteen, I was younger than most people there, and even my battle buddy, Hambrick, was about twenty years older than me. Hambrick used to be a teacher, but he couldn't take the stress anymore, so he quit and joined the Army. (We actually would go on to be in each other's faces for a while, as we were stationed in the same places for the next four years, from basic training to AIT, to our first duty station!)

Hambrick was way older than me and had lived a good bit of life already, so to have him coming to me for advice and asking me questions helped me understand that I was more mentally capable than I thought I was. A lot of the perceptions I had developed about myself in my childhood without even realizing it, from the Bethels to my uncle Omar and aunt Jackie, to my experience in the homeless shelter, were slowly but surely being broken down and replaced with who I really was.

With this new confidence, I started to love basic training. And to make things even better, my platoon began to outshine the other three platoons, and the drill sergeant who threatened me with jail that first day hated it! I didn't know how deep it was for him until he confronted me about it.

He waited until my drill sergeants had gone home one

day, came to me, and said, "Hey, Private Harris. I see what you're doing with your platoon, and I'm gonna be honest with you. I like it, I really do. So here's what I wanna do, I want you to come to my platoon and be the platoon guide in my platoon."

My platoon was the 2nd platoon, and even though I had started off rocky, by the time I got into the swing of things, I had my platoon looking like a unified group in a short period. When we'd come out, we'd call cadences that no one else was doing—basically, we just shitted on everyone else and made them look bad, and it showed. Even the other drill sergeants would kind of look back at their platoons like something was wrong with them!

This drill sergeant had noticed and was trying to steal me away from my platoon. Now, he was an infantry guy and a little bit old fashioned, so he didn't like having females in his platoon and was trying his best to get nothing but guys. My platoon had both guys and ladies, and I was perfectly happy where I was at. But when he asked me, I played it cool and said, "OK, drill sergeant, I'll think about it."

All along, I knew I wasn't going to even give him a second thought. By this time, I had become tight with my drill sergeants like they were an older brother and sister, or an uncle and aunt. They were taking me under their wing and teaching me all these things, and I was doing my best to pass it all on to our platoon. When they came in the next morning, I told them what happened, so I guess they went to the infantry drill sergeant and got on him, "Ah, so you trying to steal our best person, huh!"

He didn't say anything else to me until another day when he was walking by our classroom as I was teaching a section. He slowed down, looked in, and called out to me, "Private Harris!"

"Yes, drill sergeant!"

He pointed the finger at me with confidence and said, "I'ma get you."

Since my drill sergeants already knew, and I didn't want to leave my platoon, I didn't think too much about it and just kept doing what I was doing.

Things were going great: I was platoon guide, my platoon was outshining the others, and my drill sergeants were teaching me everything they knew. So, of course, this was the perfect time for my first dose of a reality check of being in the military.

One day, two guys in my platoon got into a fight, a black guy and a white guy, and the black guy punched the white guy in the eye. Some of the other guys ran to get me because since I was the platoon guide, I was the one responsible for handling the situation. Out of thirty people who make up a platoon, there were about twenty-five of us guys, and now we're all crammed into this small bathroom trying to figure out what's going on. Everybody's talking at once, trying to tell their version of what happened while the two guys are just sitting there bawling.

The white guy looks up at me and says, "Harris, I don't wanna get kicked out, man, I use this to send my money back to my mom and my grandmother, and they depend on me." The black guy was from Chicago, so he tells me straight up, "Man, the judge told me if I get in trouble again, I'm going to prison..."

So now, as if the pressure of fixing the situation wasn't enough, I was feeling the weight of their personal situations, too.

One thing they preach in the military is the importance of looking out for each other and having each other's backs. So, as platoon guide, I put together a quick plan.

That day they had us with our weapons and had been smoking us, making us run up and down the stairs as we carried them. We had to turn them in, so we all knew the drill sergeants were going to see this huge black eye on the white guy's face. Everybody's giving their ideas and wondering what we're going to do to avoid getting in trouble when it hits me.

"Hey, remember when they were smoking us? Just say that you got too close to somebody when they were swinging their gun, and the butt hit you in the eye."

All around the room, everyone agreed that was the best excuse, and we leave the bathroom. A couple of minutes later the drill sergeants call us downstairs, we line up in formation, and we march over to take our guns and turn them into the arms room. It's still freezing cold on the base, and we all have on our winter gear that covers our heads, so it was easy to hide as we marched. But to turn in our weapons, we have to go up one by one and walk past the drill sergeants on the way out.

Since I'm the platoon guide, I turn my weapon in first and then come back outside, and the rest of my platoon follows after me, one by one.

I'm standing outside in position waiting on my platoon when I hear one of our drill sergeants yell from inside the arms room, "PRIVATE HARRIS! GET YO' ASS IN HERE!"

I take off running back inside, but I stop short when I see all the drill sergeants standing the black guy, and the white guy, who is now crying again. My drill sergeant, who was a woman, asked me calmly, "Private Harris. What happened to this soldier's eye?"

Keeping up with our story, I replied to her with the straightest face I could hold, "Drill sergeant, when I noticed the solider's eye I asked him what happened, and he told me that when we were running up and down the stairs, somebody's butt of their gun hit him in his eye."

She looks around, and I'm trying to look at both of the guys out the corner of my eye while still facing the drill sergeants, and what I see is making my stomach slowly drop. The black guy is subtly shaking his head like, *NO, abort, abort. They know the truth*!

Without me knowing, they had already snitched!

My drill sergeant spoke again, "Private Harris, I'm gonna ask you one more time. What happened to this soldier's eye?"

Without budging an inch, I told the same story. All the drill sergeants look at me one more time, and then they tell me to get my ass outside.

I line back up with my platoon, and we march over to our barracks. I'm thinking that we've avoided the worst thing that could have happened, which was the sergeants finding out the truth and kicking out those two guys.

Instead, our drill sergeants get us to our classroom and sit us all down to talk to us. They start talking to us, and my female drill sergeant says to me, "Private Harris, you are no longer the platoon guide."

Just like that, my position is gone, and I am furious.

They continue talking, but instantly I shut down. I lean myself against the wall in the back of the classroom and don't participate at all. Typically I was always involved and speaking up, but I got so quiet, after about thirty minutes my male drill sergeant asked me what was wrong with me. "You got something to say?"

"Can I speak freely?" I responded.

"Yeah, go on and say what you need to say."

So I told them how I thought it was messed up for me to get my position taken away from me for trying to do what they always taught us, which was to look out for each other. "What are you supposed to do in my position when two people come to you over a mistake they made? One's crying about getting kicked out and not being able to send money to his family, the other's one's crying because he doesn't want to go to prison...so what are you supposed to do? We came up with a story that—"

My female drill sergeant, whom I found out later, was passionate about this because she was a medic, interrupted me. "Yeah, y'all came up with a story, but what you don't realize is that this soldier's eye could've been permanently damaged."

That was the furthest thing from my mind as a soldier in training. I had seen plenty of black eyes in the hood, but I had never seen anybody go blind for life from it! All I was thinking about was how to protect these two guys from getting kicked out of training.

I kept going off about it. "Y'all ask us not to be blue falcons..."

A blue falcon in the military is a buddy fucker, which pretty much means that you're a snitch. In my eyes, all we were trying to do was cover each other, which was what they taught us; in their eyes, we were putting a fellow solider in potential danger.

We went back and forth, saying our piece, but the bottom line was the same: I wasn't platoon guide any more. The crazy thing about the whole incident is that from that point, our platoon went downhill. We went from being the platoon that people wanted to be, to people wondering what happened to us. We faded so fast it was unbelievable.

As a platoon guide, I was used to making sure everyone did their chores and dealing with personal problems at the end of the night, and by the time I tried to take a shower, the water was usually cold. So, I started having the fire guard from the late-night shift wake me up early so I could take my shower in the morning. Now, even though I wasn't platoon guide anymore, the schedule I had developed stuck with me, and I still was getting up early before everyone was scheduled to. It wasn't a big deal; my drill sergeants knew, and I wasn't bothering anybody.

What I didn't know is that a lot of people had been complaining and writing letters that we weren't getting enough sleep, so the Command Sergeant Major of the base had put out that all soldiers would get eight hours of sleep. With me being so fresh to the military, I still wasn't familiar with rankings or anything like that, but the CSM was the officer who was in charge of making sure everything ran the way it supposed to on the base. What he said was literally law.

So one particular morning, I'm in the shower, and the drill sergeant who kept saying he was going to "get me" came up to the door and called out, "Hey, who's in here?"

Our regular wakeup time was at 6 a.m., but I was getting up at 5:45 a.m. to shower, and technically according to what the CSM had put out, I was getting up fifteen minutes too early.

Still not thinking too much about what I was doing, I called back out to him, "Private Harris."

"OH, Private Harris?"

"Yes, drill sergeant."

"When you get out of here, get your battle buddy and come see me."

"Alright, drill sergeant."

It's early, and I'm still not thinking too hard about anything, because as far as I knew, I hadn't done anything wrong. So I finish showering, grab one of the fire guards to walk downstairs with me, and the drill sergeant is standing there, rubbing his hands together, looking like a cat who just caught a mouse. "Yeah, yeah. I told you I was gonna get you, huh?"

I'm still confused, so I just say, "Yes, drill sergeant."

He starts to explain his master plan. "Yeah, so remember when the CSM put out that all soldiers would get eight hours of sleep?"

At this point, I really don't remember at all. "Yes, drill sergeant."

"Yeah, so the fact that you were up before 6 a.m., you disobeyed a direct order."

And he goes on to start telling me all these different things he's going to do to me to punish me, but I still don't have a good idea of how badly I've messed up, or how much trouble I could be in.

My drill sergeants come in later that morning around 8 o'clock, I tell them what happened, and they reassure me, "Harris, he's just mad. Don't worry about it. We'll talk to him." But next thing I know, three days later they come to me and tell me, "Hey, Private Harris, so what you're gonna do is the commander is gonna call you in, you're gonna knock on the door..."

Because I broke the eight hours of sleep rule by fifteen minutes, I was getting an Article 15 (a type of military reprimand...think getting written up by your boss, but more intense) for disobeying a direct order from a non-commissioned officer! I was placed on fifteen days restriction and fifteen days extra duty, where I was restricted to the barracks and put on cleaning duty. When I would typically have personal time after our instructional time in class, I had to go back to clean our classrooms and different things we used during the day.

Now, for the third time since I've been in training, it seems like the system has screwed me over, and I'm even more pissed off! The chaplain's taking everybody to the bowling alley, and since I've been restricted to the barracks, I'm the only soldier that can't go.

The only silver lining to being restricted to the barracks and having to clean is the classroom that we learned in had vending machines, so one day I took my change and bought something out of the vending machine. Nobody was there at night to check in to see exactly what I was doing, so it became my little thing to do at the end of every night. When I finished, the drill sergeant would tell me just to throw my trash away, go upstairs, and get in bed. They didn't pay any attention to me.

So when I started noticing nobody was really paying attention to me like that, I started with just the guys in my room first.

"Hey, listen, I'm over there with the vending machines, so I can buy us snacks..."

I'm bringing snacks back to my room every day, and word starts spreading. So now everybody starts coming to me with orders, and that same entrepreneurial spirit springs up in me with an idea: if I'm going to be risking trouble, then I need to be getting $0.50 on top of the $1 they give me to buy snacks. Nobody flinched, and the whole floor started getting in on it!

It didn't matter what was in the vending machine. I was cleaning it out every night. We'd been in basic training for weeks, and they didn't let us have anything even remotely sweet to eat, so everyone was happy with whatever I could manage to bring back! What made it even funnier was that we all had to see that vending machine when we sat in class, and whoever worked in that building had to notice what was going on because it was filled back up with snacks every day. We'd be in class cracking up to the point where our drill sergeants would start smoking us, but nobody ever gave up the secret.

But despite the little trip-ups here and there, I graduated from basic training, went straight to AIT at Fort Jackson in South Carolina to learn about my personnel role, and I was put into more leadership positions by the drill sergeants there. Just like when I was platoon guide, I found myself out in front teaching. After that, I left and was stationed at Fort Campbell in Kentucky, which made me upset because it was right down the street from Louisville, the very place I was trying to get away from. I was ready to go to Hawaii, Germany, ...anywhere in the world but back home! That was the whole point of me joining the Army in the first place.

Once I got to Fort Campbell, though, and I started learning about the base's military heritage, its traditions, and the 101st Airborne's importance because of what they did, I fell in love with it. I got the same enthusiasm back I first had during my first few days of training; I could see myself shooting up through the ranks and being a twenty-year soldier.

Everywhere I went, I made sure to excel, whether it was athletic or academic. I joined the All-Army track team (even though it was disbanded a month later), I went to AAS—anything I could do to help myself fast-track, I did.

Being stationed at Fort Campbell is also what allowed me to connect with my son's mom, Connie. A month before I joined the military when I was staying with my friend Kev and his brother, I had gone out to a club one night and met Connie. We spent a lot of time together in the month leading up to me leaving, but I wasn't sure that I'd ever see her again. So, when I was stationed so close to home, it was like we just fell back in sync with each other. It wasn't much longer before we got married, and even though we were struggling a bit to make ends meet, it seemed like things were setting in place: I had a stable career, stable wife, and a son on the way. Life was good.

7

TRUST

One thing about the Army is there's sort of an understood incentive of having a family. If you're married instead of single, you'll get more benefits. On top of your pay, the Army gives you a BAH and a BAS, which is basically just an allowance for housing and food. If you're married and you have kids, there's even more of that available to you. So, when me and Connie got back together when I got to Fort Campbell, I had the thought of, *we're already together so I might as well accept the money and just get married.*

Connie already had a son from a previous relationship, and only a month into us being married, we found out she was pregnant with my son, Devron. It was a lot quicker than either one of us anticipated, and we were struggling. I was only a PV2 at the time and was living check to check, so when I found out about deployment and how much more money we could make, I jumped on it. This was before 9/11, and the US wasn't fighting a specific war at the time, so deployments were only six months back then.

I volunteered and told Connie the benefit of it: I would be making more money and have the opportunity to stack checks in our savings. This is what I was aiming for now that I had a consistent income, but it was put in my head even more by my Grandmama Lib to try to save money. The last time I had spent time with her was when I was seven, even though I did see her a few times when I was in high school.

But when I went to her house in Louisville to get Dontoya so she could stay with my wife while I was deployed, we talked, and Grandmama Lib gave me advice that I've never forgotten, even to this day.

She simply said, "Baby, I don't care what you do. I don't care if it's $50, or even if it's $5. Just save something."

This was my whole goal for the deployment: to save up money for my family. By this point, Connie's son Kizhan was about two years old, and she just had Devron. With Dontoya there, who was eighteen years old and agreed to stay with her, I figured Connie would have the help she needed with our two young kids while I was gone. They got along well with each other, almost too well, and I guess that made what happened next so easy.

Over the next six months, Connie and my little sister pretty much tore down everything that I had built. $30,000 of debt stacked up from her not paying bills, writing bad checks, letting Dontoya drive, and total my car...it was crazy how she just made one bad move after another.

By the time I was supposed to be coming back, somehow, she got the idea that I was going to be stationed in Germany. I really think it was just because she wanted to go to Germany, being half-German herself, and so she took both Kizhan and Devron there without giving me a heads up or anything.

I had saved $10,000 while I was overseas, but when faced with the mess I came back to, it was like I came back with nothing. Most of our things were in storage, my car was wrecked, and my wife and kids were in another country.

Things were in complete financial disarray, and I wasn't happy at all. I was still married to Connie and didn't want to call it quits with her so quickly, but I knew deep down that I couldn't keep doing this with her.

One day while my family was still in Germany, I woke up to see that the $10,000 I had saved was gone! I called Connie only to find out she had taken the money and had used it as a down payment on a German car, one that we couldn't even bring back to the states if we wanted to.

This was the last straw. She was a few years older than me, and the fact that she was making these types of decisions didn't make any sense to me. How was I supposed to build a better life when the person who was supposed to help hold things together was literally tearing things down?

It was a hard realization to come to, but I knew I didn't

want to keep doing life this way with her, so we separated. To make things worse, I found out while we were separated that she was still legally married to her first son's father, so my marriage to Connie hadn't even been legal the whole time we were together.

Things were changing so quickly that my head was spinning, but I was pretty much resigned to the fact it was over with her. What really concerned me now was Devron. I had so many questions: *Would he resent me as he got older? Would he hate me because I wasn't with his mom?* My finances were a mess, and my emotions were just as jacked up.

One night I just cried because all I wanted to do was build a great life for both Kizhan and Devron, and it seemed like Connie was fighting against me at every turn no matter what I tried to do. I expected so much more from her because I had put my all into our relationship. Even though we had both been kind of doing our own thing for some months before we got together, when we finally decided to get married, I was all in.

So, to find out she wasn't whom she seemed to be, was earth-shattering. On top of already being married, realizing that she allowed herself to be mentally maneuvered into one bad decision after another by an eighteen-year-old caused me to lose all faith in her as a woman. Even considering how much time and love I had put into our relationship, I knew that type of instability wasn't what I wanted for my sons as they grew up.

In the wake of this emotional and financial disaster

was when I met another woman in the military, named Shana. She was in a relationship, and I was still on the fence trying to figure out precisely what to do with Connie, but we started spending time together and getting close.

Shana was a breath of fresh air because here was a woman who was younger than Connie but already had her life together in ways that I was working towards. She had goals in life, and that was something that resonated with me. The more time Shana and I spent together, the more I realized that Connie looked really good to me at the beginning of our relationship because of the low point I was at in life when I met her.

As I was starting my career in the Army, I didn't think it was the be-all-end-all solution for my life. I was glad to be in a stable position, but I wanted to go higher from there, not just stay in a month-to-month paycheck cycle. Probably because she had been raised with her dad in the military, Connie thought as long as you were in the military, things were fine. Even if we blew through finances and there was no real change in our status, as long as paychecks were coming in every month, she was satisfied. To me, it was just another trap of a cycle, and I was done being content with staying in someone else's system for my life.

Once the truth about her was revealed, it was like I had an epiphany: she wasn't as good for me as I thought, and she was actually holding me back.

After that realization, it wasn't hard to make a decision, and things with Shana started going great. I was determined not to repeat the mistakes I had made with Connie, so I took everything terrible that had happened and learned from it. Before we could get in too deep with each other, I sat Shana down and told her straight up, "Hey, if you trust in me, I promise you, we'll never live check to check. We'll have an amazing life, just believe in me that I want better for us."

So now here I was, $30,000 in debt and determined to flip things around. I got an unexpected teacher in the lady who worked for the car company that repossessed my car, and she ended up teaching me things about credit that I had never heard of. Over the course of two years, I kept meeting people just like the lady from the car company who taught me things about money and how to get myself back on track. I soaked it all up like a sponge.

During that time, Shana allowed me to use my paychecks to pay off all the debt that Connie had put me in, while she pretty much took care of all our other expenses. She was just as scared as I was at the time, and my promise probably seemed the furthest thing from the truth. But one thing I can say is Shana trusted me. I did my best to reassure her that I wouldn't steer us wrong, and she really worked together with me. At the age of nineteen, we got her credit score to 700, and when she saw that, I think it really settled the idea that we were headed in the right direction together.

We got married, and life started taking off even more. I started my first business and bought my first home while we were together, and those things I used to long for and pick out of the newspaper as a kid: houses, cars, shoes, food...all those things started to become an everyday reality for me.

Up until this time in my life, I had never really had anyone stable who was around me long enough to show me what to do and not to do when it came to setting up my life for success as an adult. Unlike with Connie, it was the first time that I had a whole family of in-laws who were around and active in my life. Shana had a huge family full of relatives, and just being around them showed me what it meant to be more family-oriented.

After I got out of debt and things started turning around, we were doing so well that we were saving $30,000 a year, traveling, and doing things that most people our age were still dreaming about. We became the couple that everybody wanted to be like. Little girls would tell their moms, "When I grow up, I wanna have a relationship like Rob and Shana!"

Things were good financially and materially, but during our marriage, I started to realize there were parts of me that weren't me in our relationship. While I wasn't completely miserable, I noticed that she seemed to care about other people's thoughts and opinions more than mine, and it started to have a quiet effect on me.

Still, for the first time in my life, I was experiencing what it meant to be financially and emotionally free to a certain extent, and I was loving it.

8

99 PROBLEMS BUT A B**** AIN'T ONE

At the age of twenty-two, things finally seemed to be going right for me. My Army career was progressing steadily, I had gotten out of debt and was saving money like nobody's business, I was married to a woman who was on board with my goals in life, and I had gained a whole family in the process. Now, with a more solid foundation under my feet, I was able to start looking beyond day-to-day surviving and plan ahead more.

I was about four years into my enlistment and was coming up on deciding whether or not I wanted to reenlist. At the beginning of my term, my mind was set on making a career in the Army. I had focused on moving up through the ranks fast, and I had. But after seeing people make more money than I was while deployed and exploring other opportunities like starting a business, I wasn't too sure about that decision anymore.

While I was on that six month deployment when

Connie and I were together, I had been making around $14,000, which included the bonus I was getting. To me, that was great money; anything more than what I was making at home was worthwhile!

But one day, while I was checking in contractors, I met a young kid who was only nineteen years old, and he told me he was making $89,000!

My jaw dropped as he told me he was working with his uncle, who was the foreman for the contractor company that was working for the Army. After that day, the gears in my head started turning. Why would I continue to work in the Army and make what now looked like a drop in the bucket, when I could work for the Army, have more freedom, and make a crapload more of a check?

It seemed like a no-brainer to me!

Even watching how Shana's dad created his business motivated me to change how I thought about myself. It allowed me to see that I didn't have to always be working for somebody else, and I could create my own business, too!

I had to weigh my decision a little bit more, but while I was doing that, Shana ended up getting orders to go to Alaska.

By this point, we had gotten way more invested with each other. We had been living together, doing big things, and it was pretty safe to say that I loved her. On my part, I had officially decided to leave the Army, but since we weren't married yet, that was making things harder.

When you're in the Army, love just isn't enough; you

have to be official in their eyes! They had already sent her to Alaska, but since I wasn't her husband and I wasn't reenlisting, I couldn't automatically go with her. Also, all of our furniture and household goods were mine, so when she left, she couldn't take any of those things with her. So now I was faced with another choice: do I marry this girl?

The answer looked clear to me then—YES!

We got married quick, I packed up everything, and now I was just waiting to be shipped off to Alaska.

Now before I left, I had been talking with some of my family off and on, and one day my uncle Joe told me out of the blue, "Hey Rob, man, I saw your dad on the bus!"

"What, my dad?"

"Nah, for real! If I see him again, you want me to get his number for you?"

I didn't care too much about it, so I just told him, "Yeah, you know, that's cool."

At this point, I was twenty-two years old and had never met the man in my life. I wasn't excited or expecting anything special, but I did always wonder what he looked like because growing up, people were always telling me all these stories about who he was.

My grandmother would tell me he was so tall, "When your dad came through that door, he had to bend down!" Camp would straight up lie to me about him; he even told me one time that my dad played for the University of Louisville! As a young kid, I wasn't about to keep that to myself, so I went to my school extra proud and told my teacher about my dad. Of course, she asked me what his name was, and I told her. I guess she went home and looked in some books to try to find him, but obviously, she couldn't. When we came back to school the next day, she told me she couldn't find him, and at that point, we were both confused! It probably should've been real clear after that, but it took years to go by before I found out Camp was lying.

All these different stories and accounts about who he was (and who he wasn't) really built up a desire in me to just know who he was for myself.

About two weeks had passed when my Uncle Joe called me and told me he saw my dad and got his number. So he gives it to me, I call him, and my dad picks up.

Straight to the point, I say, "Hey, I'm Rob."

My dad sounds excited to hear from me, and tells me, "Oh man, come see me! You have a brother..."

That's news to me, so I decide to take him up on it. Biddle, one of my boys in the military, told me he would roll with me for support, so I went down to Louisville that weekend to meet my biological father for the first time.

Spoiler alert: it wasn't what I expected.

If you've ever seen the movie *Hustle and Flow*, that's what it looked like when I walked into his house. The only thing missing was the soundtrack. He had some random white girl in there, and I didn't actually see any drugs, but they looked like they had just finished doing something. The house was filthy, the girl was looking sluttish and dirty, my dad's shirt was hanging open, and he was looking dirty—it was like meeting two crackheads.

But still, all I could think in my head was, *this is the dude who told the state that he didn't want me.*

When I was younger, Camp and I were in court with our social worker because our mom was losing us. The court had asked our grandma if she wanted us, but she said no. She had taken care of almost everyone in our family at some point, and I think she couldn't take anymore.

We were about to get on the elevator to leave the courthouse with our social worker and grandma when a thought popped up in my head.

I asked my social worker, "Hey, did y'all hear from my daddy?"

I never forgot my social worker's face when she told me, "No, no, we...we didn't find him."

Our social worker was one of those people whom you could tell what they really meant by the look on her face, and I knew she was lying to try to protect my feelings. It was never officially confirmed, but I just felt that they found him, and my dad had told them no, he didn't want me.

I never forgot that lie all those years ago, and finally seeing my father was like putting a new face to that old lie.

Meeting him showed me what type of man I didn't want my son to see. I knew I never wanted to take my son down here and say, "Hey, this is your grandfather!" There was just nothing I saw in him that I wanted to keep in my life. At that moment, I made peace with the fact that after this weekend, I knew I was never going to see or speak to him again.

The bittersweet thing about this decision was that I did meet the brother my dad had told me about, but I knew cutting off contact with my dad meant that I would lose contact with my brother Rob. (Our moms both named us after our dad, so not only were we both named Rob, we were both the 3rd, since we got his exact name.)

I wasn't exactly happy about it, but it just seemed like part of the price to pay.

When the weekend was over, before I pulled off, I gave my dad the cell phone number that I knew I was getting ready to cut off when I moved to Alaska. The only thing I really wanted was to show him that I made it without him.

Since that was done, there was nothing else left to hold on to, so I let him go.

That was around the end of 2002, and I didn't hear from him or anyone on his side of the family until about 2008 when I found out that my dad had died.

One of my cousins I met when I went down there to meet my dad was in the military too, but he had gone AWOL for a while. They eventually got him back in, and he was the one who looked me up on the military email account system to tell me the news. I reached out to my aunt, who was my dad's sister and went down there after the funeral. That's how I ended up getting back in touch with my brother Rob since I had cut him off when I cut off my dad those years before.

When I got to Louisville, the first thing my aunt asked

me was, "You know, I got this much left to pay for the funeral, can you pay it?"

All I could think was, *wow, I didn't even know this, man.*

Even to this day, I don't even let Rob call him my dad. We'll be talking, and he'll say easily, "Yeah man, 'cause our dad...", and I'll cut him off before he can finish, "Rob, that's your dad, that's not my dad." My brother Rob had him in his life off and on, but I never saw or heard from him until I was twenty-two.

The way I felt about it then, and now, was real simple: that guy was not my dad.

Even though it wasn't what I expected, I finally got some closure on that part of my life. I didn't know it, but it would only be a few years later that I would be able to get closure in another significant way.

In 2010, I found out my grandmother had colon cancer and had been hiding it for a long time. By this time, I had been in Alaska for eight years and had become the successful one in the family, and the only one who I really talked to on this side was my grandmother. She had retired, and I would just buy her different things that I knew she liked. Fish was one of the things she loved, and being in Alaska I was able to send her all types of different fish she wouldn't have found down there in Kentucky. I didn't have my mom, so my grandmother became the one that I really spoiled and took care of.

She was happy to see me doing well and that my attitude about life had gotten more positive. Every time she got a chance, she would brag on me, but it just made the whole family hate me even more! Even though years had passed, and I was an adult, my family was still holding on to whatever grudge they had against me even as a kid.

Everything happened so fast that, one day, I was talking with her like everything was fine, and the next thing I knew, the Red Cross was sending me a message telling me she was in the hospital with hours to live. Immediately I took emergency leave to fly my family and me down to Louisville, and when we got there, I saw Aunt Jackie and Uncle Omar in the hospital room. I also met another aunt, one of my grandmother's daughters, whom she had never talked much about before.

Every day we were up at the hospital, it was like we were playing the worst waiting game in the world. We knew my grandmother was going to pass soon, but she was still able to talk with us, so we were just trying to make the most of the little time we knew was left.

We were all up at the hospital one day: me, my grandmother, Aunt Jackie, Uncle Omar, my aunt, whom I had just met, and my wife. While everyone was talking, I made a small comment, "When grandmama pass, there really won't be a need for me to come back to Louisville anymore because I really only came to see her."

Aunt Jackie seemed to take it personally, because she stood up and started walking in my face, saying, "Oh, so that's the reason, Ramon? That's why we don't see you, why you all closed off and don't nobody ever hear from you?"

As calmly as I could still sitting in my seat, I looked straight at her and said, "Aunt Jackie, listen. You're my aunt, and I love and respect you, but get out of my face."

She backed up, and I repeated what I said. There was nothing for me to come back to: Camp was strung out, Anthony was in prison, Dontoya was ghost, and I had no idea where Sheronda was. The last time I had even tried to look for her was in 2002 right before I moved to Alaska, and before that, the last time I even saw her was when she was five years old.

None of my cousins and I talked to each other, and the rest of my family just seemed to be drug-infested, so what was there really to come back to?

Then Uncle Omar said, "See, that's the problem right there, 'cause if you wanna keep it real, I'm the reason you successful today."

"What?" I said.

"Yeah, that's right," he said with a smirk on his face, "when you came to my house you were making D's and F's, but I'm the one who pushed you to get good grades to get on the honor roll and everything."

This guy...I couldn't believe he really had the boldness to tell that lie in front of everybody!

"No," I replied, "no, you got me fucked up. That was Camp who was making D's and F's. I was already a good student before I ever got to your house. And on top of that, I'm thirty. You telling me the two years I lived with you out of my life made me the man I am today? Nah, what you did was show me everything a man shouldn't do, and I made sure to never be like you."

Our voices were getting louder and louder to the point that the nurses were coming in telling us to be quiet, and my wife was doing her best to calm me down because I was just done with them.

But my grandmother, laying there in her hospital bed, was encouraging me, "No, no, Mone, say what you need to say! Y'all don't stop him from talking. Y'all don't realize how they been treating him all these years, all these years. Baby, get it off your chest, tell them what you need to tell them!"

So, I kept talking. "You want to know the reason why y'all haven't been seeing me all these years? The reason why is because I wanted to hurt y'all for what y'all did to my brother, to my family, to us—I wanted to do something to y'all. Every day, I thought about that. Y'all are the last people that stopped me from seeing my mom before she died. It was you who did that! So when I have those thoughts, all I think about is all the bad y'all did to me, and I don't want to see you!"

After I finished blowing up, Aunt Jackie was doing all this fake crying like I'd hurt her feelings by accusing her of something that never happened, and she and Uncle Omar left the hospital. The next day I was back up at the hospital with the aunt I had just met, and she encouraged me to talk to them again. "You know, they're still your family, and you should really sit down with them and have an adult conversation about all the anger you have."

It seemed like a good idea, so I called Uncle Omar and said, "Hey, I'll be at grandmama's house if you want to talk to me."

"Yeah, man," he agreed, "let's sit down and have a conversation. 'Cause you said a lot of stuff in there that hurt your aunt's feelings...."

He came over, and we sat down to have what I thought was going to be a heart-to-heart, man-to-man conversation. And to be honest, all I was really looking for from him was just an apology. An explanation would have been nice, but it wouldn't have taken back all the damage they did and all the hurt they caused my family. An apology, though, would have at least showed that they knew what they did and that it was wrong.

Instead, this dude looked me dead in my eyes and tried to convince me everything I said was a straight-up lie.

I started confronting him about everything, even my little brother. "I remember the beatings you used to give Anthony. You treated him like he was some type of fucking soldier! Why?"

But instead of apologizing, he literally told me I was making all this shit up in my head and that none of it never happened. He never whooped Anthony; the only one who ever whooped him was Aunt Jackie, and she only did it a couple of times. According to him, I was just making the whole thing up.

When he said that, what I said next was real easy to say.

"I'm done, man."

133

I ended the conversation and told myself I would never talk to that motherfucker again. And I haven't spoken to him since.

There were only so many days you could get for emergency leave, so we had to fly back while my grandmother was still in the hospital. We spent Christmas in Alaska, and the next day on December 26th, 2010, she passed away. True to what I said, it seemed like there was nothing there for me in Louisville anymore.

But one day while I was driving home from work, my phone rang. It was a lady named Dyanne, whom I went to high school within Louisville.

A few months before, I had just met with Shawanna, another old high school friend from Louisville, who had moved up to Alaska. Since she still talked to people we used to run with down in Kentucky, I told her she could pass my number to some of them. Dyanne was one of those old friends, but I was a little bit shocked when she asked me, "Hey Rob, do you have a sister?"

"Yeah, I got a couple of sisters."

"OK, well, do you have a sister named Sheronda?"

I paused a second before replying, "Yeah, I got a sister named Sheronda. Does she have pretty eyes or a scar on the side of her mouth?"

"Oh my God, Rob."

"What?"

"Your sister works for me!"

"Get the fuck out of here!" I said. After all these years of not being able to find her, man, I couldn't believe it!

She explained to me how she was walking past my sister's desk and saw an old picture of me around the time that I was in 5th grade. When she was younger, Sheronda had been adopted by a woman, Ms. Jackson, and she had always told her that she had brothers and sisters out there in Louisville, so she might run into us one day. But Ms. Jackson wouldn't let her know where we were at, and we moved around so much, Sheronda couldn't keep up with us anymore when she was looking.

When she was younger, Sheronda had gotten a copy of the picture that me, my brothers, and my mom took when we were at my sister Latoya's funeral and had kept it all those years. When Dyanne saw it on her desk, she immediately recognized me.

"I know that little boy! That's Rob. I went to high school with *him*!"

She said my little sister was so excited; she said, "Shut up, are you serious? That's my brother. I've never met him."

Dyanne told her, "I can call him. I just got his number!"

"Are you serious?"

So that's why Dyanne was calling me, and she told me, "Rob, your sister works for me, so I'm going to put her on break so she can call you."

Sheronda called me thirty minutes later, and that's how we finally got back in touch with each other.

Since 2002, I had been contacting the social services in Louisville, trying to find her, but it was always nothing but dead ends. Nobody would help me, but then a few days after my grandmother passed, I found her again. It was like one last gift from my grandmother, and it helped to know that now, I did have another reason to come back to visit Louisville.

It seemed like as soon as I decided to move to Alaska, over the twelve years I was there, I was able to bring closure to so many parts of my life that had left me questioning, "Why?" From meeting my dad to getting the anger off my chest to my aunt and uncle, to finally finding my sister again, so much healing took place in me that I really grew into whom I wanted to be as a man without all the baggage weighing me down.

Officially out of the Army now, I was in a new phase of life. I was married, no longer in the military, and looking at life differently in terms of whom I wanted to be now as a husband, father, and businessman. Learning how to move from working *in* the military to working *for* the military was a huge transition, but it was one I was determined to make. I knew more money and less stress were on the line.

I found a job working for the Department of Defense as a GS in Alaska, so even though I was still in the Guard, I actually worked *for* them as well. Things were going good: the schedule was easy, the work was easy, the pay was worth it—everything about it was great! But after a while, it just started getting old. On top of that, I still had that itch to be my own boss instead of just working for others.

On a trip to Chicago, I got my first big idea. While we were there, I was looking up things to do, and I found a touring company called Chicago Dine Around, where they took you around to all the places in the city that had some type of famous person associated with them. The thing I found cool about it was throughout the tour, they took you to three different restaurants, and you had all three parts of your meal at those different restaurants: your appetizer, your entrée, and finally your dessert.

I had a great time during the whole tour, and we thought, *why not try to do the same thing in Alaska?* Alaska's known as a very touristy state, and where we were living at the time, no one had done anything like that yet. It seemed to be really cost-effective since the only big part we had to put money into was a bus, so we decided to do it.

A private school sold its bus to us, and by the summer of 2011, we had our touring company officially up and running. We were on the radio doing interviews. We made sure our company was blasted all over the touring sites, and business was doing great!

In the middle of this success, a friend of ours started talking to us about an opportunity to own a basketball team. We did a little research on the ins and outs of it, and finally, my wife and I sat down to have a business dinner with him and his wife. Eventually, we decided to create a collaborative group of the four of us to purchase and run the team together. All four of us went in on it with different roles, but it still became very time-consuming.

I was still the driver for the touring company. However, we started to look at the revenue we were bringing in from the basketball team in comparison to what we were bringing in from the touring company, and it was pretty obvious that we were making way more from the team. On top of that, there were so many more moving parts involved in running a team, from recruiting players to setting up cheerleaders to securing a venue. It was becoming almost impossible to fit in driving tours.

So we dissolved the touring company, used that extra financial boost to support our basketball team, and the touring bus turned into the new travel bus for the team. Our team had a great first year, and we went ahead and started planning even better things for the second year. Since the first team was doing well, we went forward with a plan. We had to bring a second team to Alaska. That helped us reduce the cost of flying other teams in to play against our team, and also created a little bit of a local rivalry in the city. Some people were loyal to the "original" team, while others supported the new team since some of the players had been moved to it. At times the rivalry went a little too far, but it was good for business!

On the business side of things, it helped us divide up responsibilities even more to where one couple took care of one team while the other couple took care of the other team.

The basketball franchise continued to go well, but at the same time that I was doing that, I was still thinking about how I could get back into coaching. I didn't realize it at first, but I had become addicted to coaching.

Before starting the touring company and basketball team, I had been coaching from 2008 to 2010. The problem was, the school I was at wouldn't hire me as a head coach, but the coaches they had on staff full-time were starting to become afraid of me. Even though I was part-time to them, to me, it was my full-time passion.

I would fly myself to coaching camps, learn from other coaches I respected, and I was just always working on my craft. One thing I learned from one of those coaches was something very simple. All he said was, "Man, you can't lie to players. Players know if you telling them bullshit, and once you lose that player, you can never get them back." Some people might have let that slide, but I took advice like that seriously, and it started showing up the other coaches.

No matter what school I was at, I found myself always being the kids' favorite coach, but it just made the other coaches fearful that I was trying to take their job. That made coaching even more frustrating because I had to spend more time than I wanted trying to put out fires I hadn't even started and convincing my head coach that, hey, I was their assistant. My whole point of being there was to help us win, not make us lose, whether it was their job or a game!

Unfortunately, the coaching scene got a little crazy since, being in Alaska, there was only a small group of schools in the area. I had started to feel like I wasn't able to grow the way I wanted to in my coaching, and I realized that for me to really pursue what I wanted, I had to go to the next level, which was college. The problem with that was I had to leave Alaska to do it.

I wasn't feeling ready to do that then, and since I wasn't getting anymore coaching jobs, I had stopped in 2010 and focused on starting our businesses. They had been doing well, but coaching still never left my mind.

So now I was torn between a lot of things: our basketball team was doing great, I was tired of the GS job I was still doing for the state, and I still wanted to leave to get back into coaching and further my career. Ultimately, my wife and I made the big decision for me to leave for Charlotte, North Carolina, to live with her parents so I could get into college coaching. She would stay in Alaska for the time, and that way, we didn't have to pay rent twice.

Over four years, I had started more successful businesses than most people ever would in a lifetime, and even now, when I look back at that time in my life, I'm amazed. I had always thought about what it would be like to own my own business when I was a kid. If I could tell that little kid getting abused by his uncle and aunt what would happen, he probably would've cussed me out.

But it happened! I made it out of the rough start I'd had, the shitty relationship that almost destroyed what I was trying to build. Now, after all the successful businesses, I was finally pursuing the passion I'd always had.

TRANSITION

W hen I got to Charlotte, things were starting to
look up. The space I needed to grow as a coach
was there, unlike up in Alaska, where everything was so
closed in. I got a job pretty quickly coaching college football, and it felt like this was the way in that I had been
looking for.

But while things were looking up when it came to my
career, a serious strain was starting to show in my
marriage. My wife was still living in Alaska while I was
down at her parents' house in Charlotte, but we had been
dealing with problems before I even left. I was determined
to do my best and keep moving forward in our marriage,
but things were getting so tense, divorce was seeming like
the only option.

Besides that, I had gotten a job pretty quickly coaching
football in Charlotte, and I already had another interview
coming up to coach basketball at one of the high schools in

town. It actually went really well! All the staff liked me and wanted me to work there. The only thing that stopped me was the principal wanted me to teach a class too, and I didn't want to be a teacher, just a coach. He told me he had to hire for the needs of his school, so he gave the position to someone else.

When I didn't get the job, and it seemed like things were pretty much over between Shana and me, it looked like there was no point in me staying in Charlotte anymore. When I talked to Kev about what was going on, he opened his doors to me. "Man, come on down to Atlanta and get a fresh start."

They told me I didn't get the job on that Friday, I chilled in Charlotte over the weekend, and on Sunday, I packed up my stuff and drove down to Atlanta. After that, me and my wife got divorced.

Being in Atlanta divorced and now single, things were new, but my future was up in the air. I wasn't sure if I wanted to stay here or not, especially with Devron living in Tampa with his mom—but I decided to stay and see what Atlanta had to offer.

I knew I was going to have to work hard to build myself back up financially, but I was open to going in any direction, as long as it was a good one. I had been in the military for so long. I was always around people who were either in the military or were affiliated with the military in some way, so now that I was in Atlanta, it was like I was leaving Louisville all over again to explore the world.

Even living with Kev was something totally different.

We had been best friends since we were fourteen, but we had to kind of relearn each other because of the different paths we had walked in life. The crazy thing was we both had been successful in our own ways, and even our friend Ron told us how lucky we both were to be able to get out of that Louisville "bowl" and learn more about the world. As bad as things had gone for me lately, it really put life in perspective for me.

Atlanta was the biggest city I had ever lived in, and eventually, I came to the realization that Atlanta was a town where I would want to start a business. So I started thinking, *OK, now what do I want to start?*

The first few months, from the end of August in 2013 until about October or November, was one of the most frustrating times I had in Atlanta. I immediately started trying to find work, but nobody would hire me. I think it was because, with all my military and state experience, I was overqualified, and people wanted to underpay me. It even got to a point where I tried to get a low-paying job, but they still wouldn't hire me because of my experience. Since I couldn't get a job right away, I started living off a little of my 401k money from my Department of Defense job, and the first thing I decided to do was take myself to bartending school.

Since I was staying and Atlanta was a party town, I figured starting a lounge someday made the most sense, and I needed to know how to run a bar. Getting the training only cost about $400, so it seemed like a good investment. I don't drink at all, but I learned from the show *Bar Rescue* that the number one money-maker in any club or lounge is the bar. If you can get that straight, you'll get the sales.

I don't even drink, but I knew this was something that would help me in the long run.

But still, Kev had jokes, "How you gonna take a bartending course? You don't even drink!"

Still, I passed, and once I finished that, I found a real estate program in 2014 that was paid for by the military that lasted from February to March. Becoming a realtor was not a part of my plan, but I wanted to learn the knowledge behind it since Atlanta's housing market was booming, and I thought about how at some point in the future, I wanted to invest in realty.

Even though I wasn't getting into these businesses yet, I was taking this time to start my plan by gaining knowledge so I could rebuild brick by brick. It wasn't going to happen overnight, but I knew everything was going to come together eventually.

When I got out of real estate school, I started applying for different types of jobs, and I went to a job conference where I got a job with Norwegian Cruise Line. The hiring manager saw all the management experience I had working for the Department of Defense, and with the bartending certificate I had, he told me, "Man, here's what's crazy: I could probably get you to be the bar manager on one of the cruise lines."

I was too excited. "Shut up, are you for real?"

He shook his head, yes. "Dude, you'll make a crazy stack of money."

There was nothing else to say; I was ready to go!

Norwegian hired me, April came, and I went up to Maryland for their training. While I was in training, I started finding out the real details of the jobs.

I would have been sitting on a cruise ship circling Hawaii for six months, with a break from the ship of six weeks. On top of that, I would have had to stay in Hawaii. There was just no way I was going to be away from Devron for six months at a time, just for $30,000. That wasn't the game plan I was looking for.

Around this time, Kev's little brother, Nelly, decided he wanted to come to Atlanta too. During this time, when I came back, Kev asked me to meet a guy with him who had a business plan for a logistics company. We sat with him in his office, and listened to him, pitch us his investment deal.

The idea was a good one, and the company itself was great, but I just didn't have a good feeling about the guy we met with.

When we left the meeting, I told Kev, "Listen, the plan he has is great. I don't know anything about logistics right now, but we can learn it. Then we should do it ourselves, not go through him!"

Kev was down with it immediately, "Alright, let's put the plan in play."

So I told him my plan: first, we needed to go to truck-driving school to get CDLs.

Kev wasn't hearing it. He had an offshore job making $115k a year, and going to school for a CDL seemed like a waste of time.

Since Nelly was in Atlanta now, me and him left to go to CDL school in May 2014.

We got to Iowa on June 1st, and we immediately started training for three weeks for CRST at one of the local colleges. They put us up in a little rinky-dink hotel that had bed bugs and everything! They were feeding us one meal a day, but we were already pretty much broke, so I was eating $1 biscuits from McDonald's every morning. Anything I could find that was cheap to make, like spaghetti, I was making it!

Finally, we graduated and started driving for the company. But in exchange for them paying for my truck-driving school, I had to drive for the company first to pay off the debt.

The whole time I was there, I only had one purpose in mind: to learn the business. I already had ten plus years of HR experience, state-level experience when it came to management, so I wasn't concerned about the personnel side. I just needed to know how to drive and what all the ins and outs of trucking were. The only downside of all of this was I had to sacrifice what I would be making, and all the time, it was going to take me to pay them back.

I was literally making only $0.25 a mile, so me, Nelly, and some other guys I met, Cory and Brian, started trying to figure out how we could leave the company. Cory was from Atlanta, and Brian was kind of from the Macon area, so I got one of my friends from Atlanta to come pick all of us up in Iowa.

On the way back, we were all talking about how we were going to find a better paying company, and I straight up told them about how my whole plan was to drive just long enough until I could open my own business.

Cory took me seriously and told me, "Hey, man, when you do, call me. I'll work for you!"

So we got back to Atlanta, and the first thing I did was get online to try to find us a new trucking company to work for. Now we that had our CDLs, we were supposed to work for CRST for eight months at $0.25 a mile to pay off our training, and then either our pay would go up, or we could leave to a different company.

The problem was when you first start trucking, a lot of companies won't hire you if you don't have any driving time, which we didn't know. Plus, a lot of lawsuits had been happening because of poaching, where one company would train you, and then another company would "steal" you by hiring you, already trained. Because of that, a lot of companies were scared of getting sued and wouldn't hire us.

We finally found one company that would hire us, and they sent all four of us over to do the drug test. Everybody passed the drug test, but me because for this test, they took hair from our underarms—and I didn't have enough!

I had done all of our resumes and everything, and everybody else got hired but me, all because I can't grow underarm hair!

Ultimately, I had to bite the bullet and go back to the company I just ran from. They put me on a Greyhound all the way back to Iowa, did my refresher training, and I went to Oklahoma to go with my trainer on the road.

From the beginning of June, I drove for them all the way until the beginning of November, but during those five months, I still kept my plan in mind of learning the business.

I never made more than $1,000 a month while I was learning, but that's what I was living off of. The apartment I had was a struggle to pay for, and by the time I took care of rent and the little utilities I was using, I was living off almost $100 for the whole month. Eventually, the rental office told me I couldn't even renew my lease because I was always paying my rent late. I was eating ramen noodles, Vienna sausages, spaghetti—whatever I could buy, that would be as cheap as possible.

One day Nelly talked to me about getting on with a railroad company that one of his friends told him about. He said it was good money, so while I was still driving, I applied for the railroad company and got an interview scheduled up in North Dakota. Nelly had his eyes set on going to a big city like Chicago or Indianapolis, but me? I couldn't care less; I just needed a job. I was willing to go anywhere, as long as I was getting paid. Plus, I figured most people didn't want to go to North Dakota, so I would have a better chance of getting hired.

So, I called my dispatcher to route me through North Dakota so I could make it to the interview—but she had sent me all the way over to Ohio, so by the time I got there from doing my route, I missed it. Luckily the guy at the company emailed somebody and told me they another interview for me, and this time, I wasn't going to miss it.

This time I did a few more loads and quit CRST so I could make it to the interview, but my dispatcher called me. "Robert, why are you leaving us?"

I just told her the truth, "You know, I just can't work on this type of pay and support my family."

"Well, why didn't you talk to me?"

I knew she had a kid, so I just talked to her straight up. "Don't you have a young kid?"

"Yeah."

"Ok, well, I've been here for five months, and in five months, I haven't made more than $1,000 a month. Can you take care of a family on that?"

She couldn't answer me, but I knew she knew the answer was no.

"Exactly ma'am, you know you couldn't take care of your family on that, so how can you expect me to take care of my family on that?"

She tried to threaten me a little bit about the company coming after me, but I didn't care—I knew this was just the next step in my plan.

The railroad company ended up hiring me, and they told me I had to be in North Dakota by November 17th. So I drove back to Atlanta to pack up all my stuff and got back on the road to North Dakota. This was a 3,000-mile trip I was making every time, but it didn't matter to me. One of my tires even went flat on the way up there, so I had the ride my donut the whole way from Tennessee to North Dakota at 53 miles an hour—but still, I was just happy I was making moves forward.

Once I made it there and got settled in, I started the four-month training and passed it, but then we got laid off almost a week or two after graduating the training in March 2015.

So I packed everything up again and drove all the way back down to Atlanta. I still had my apartment, but now it was me, Nelly, and some other dudes we had met from Atlanta, and we're all trying to get jobs. A couple of weeks went by, and things were doing ok. I had saved some money while I was up there for the four months, and the railroad company told us they would probably call us back.

But while I was looking for a job and waiting for the railroad company to call me back, I got into a car accident. I didn't want to spend all the money it would take to get the car repaired, and I figured, man, I only got one life.

So I went and bought a 2016 Audi A7, brand new, right off the showroom floor.

Everybody thought I had lost my mind. "Dude, you just got laid off, and you go buy a brand new $80,000 car?"

"Man, I don't even care no more, I'm just about to go live life!"

The railroad company finally called us back in June, but it wasn't for me to work as a conductor. Instead, they had me working in Cedar Rapids, Iowa fixing railroad tracks for Maintenance Away in the summer all the way through to winter. By this point, I was making almost $12,000 a month, stacking up more money. I knew it was going to come to an end, but at the same time, they were telling me that eventually, they were going to bring me back as a conductor.

I did that from June to December 2015 before they laid us off, again!

This time I had saved up a good bit of money, so I wasn't caught off-guard like the other times they laid me off. But I was expecting them to call me back, so I did something that came back to bite me: I loaned a friend $20,000.

Bad mistake.

The railroad company still didn't have a job for me, and I was waiting, waiting, waiting—

During these months, I was pretty much homeless, staying with a friend in the basement of their house. Devron had come back from Florida to live with me, and even though I was living off my savings account, I knew I needed something to happen.

It was just us now, and even though I considered myself to be pretty good at saving money, when nothing is coming in, it still drains pretty quick. I finally managed to get an apartment in February 2016. By the time April 2016 came, I was tapped out. I was paying my car payment late, my son was playing AAU basketball, and other bills were still coming. I knew I had to get a job soon. In May, I got hired on with Greyhound.

Greyhound ended up hiring me as a bus driver, but I was having a problem with their bus seats. For some reason, their seats were killing my back, and I already had back issues, so I had to take off after only a couple of months because of a back injury. Once that happened, I knew I had to find employment again, and soon.

In my search, I found out I could apply for railroad unemployment since apparently railroads laying people off frequently was more common than I knew. I qualified for it since I had been laid off from my conductor position for two years, and it finally kicked in. That lasted me until October 2016, and I applied for a job with AT&T in the same month. The problem was their hiring process was so long, I didn't actually get hired until January 2017.

As soon as I got ready to start with AT&T on the first day of the job, I found myself with sciatica. I literally couldn't even walk for almost a month! I was crawling around my house, couldn't work at all, and AT&T had me on some type of leave until I could get to work. I was still living off the little money I had saved, but the sciatica seemed like it was getting even worse.

The railroad called me out of nowhere and asked me to come back, but this time I would have to move to Montana. They wanted me to come in March, so I took that job because it gave me more time to get recover instead of waiting in limbo with AT&T. I was able to start walking around and get myself back together in enough time to start with the railroad in March, and I did that until they laid me off in October. Since my son was with me and he was in school, we didn't move back to Atlanta until January 2018 because I didn't want to interrupt his school year if I could help it.

This last time I was with the railroad company, though, I had had enough. I was sick of getting laid off by these companies over and over, so from March to October, all I did was work as much as possible, and I stacked as much money as I could. I wasn't loaning out anything! With that job and the money the military was giving me, I was able to save about $100,000 in those months.

I was determined that this time when they laid me off, I was going to start my own company.

November 2017 came, and the railroad company laid me off for the last time. I got with Kev, and we started doing all the paperwork and research that we needed to get started. As soon as my son ended the semester and we moved back to Atlanta, Kev and I put the plan in motion, and we've been Quake Logistics ever since then!

EPILOGUE

LIFE IS GOOD

If anyone would have asked me when I was just getting in the Army if I knew I would own a million-dollar company by the time I was forty, I probably would've laughed in their face! But after coming out one of the lowest times in my life after my divorce, even though I went through another crazy hard couple of years, that's precisely where I found myself.

The other most amazing thing that came out of this same time is that I met my now fiancée and mother of my daughter, Raven.

February 1st, 2016, on my birthday, is when I met her. When we first met, we hit it off immediately. We chilled with each other for like a week, and it was one of the best weeks of my life. The only problem was my situation at the time was so embarrassing to me. When I met her, I was living with a friend and staying in a room because I still had the Audi and bills, and I didn't have enough money to have my own crib yet.

We spent a lot of time together in that first week, but I knew that for a woman like her, I didn't have anything to offer yet. On top of that, we would fade in and out because I would have to go back to work at the railroad up north. As much as we tried to keep in contact, it was just hard because we would lose phones, change numbers—but no matter what, I would look for her. I always tried to find her, no matter what.

A few years later, when I came back from Montana after getting laid off for the last time in January 2018, I finally was starting to feel ready, in more ways than one. Me and Kev had started building our company, but we knew we had to go on the road ourselves and drive our first truck for our company.

First, I sat my son down and explained to him that I knew it was his junior year, and I was going to miss a lot of events, but I promised him I wouldn't miss anything his senior year. I was going to build this company up for us and change our lives for the better if he could just hold on for a year. He was very understanding, so with him on board, I went ahead on the road with Kev.

We drove that truck until it could drive no more! I was eating fruit cups and Vienna sausages on the road, but not because I really had to at this point, but because I wanted to. Stacking money was the main goal so we could buy more trucks, get more employees, expand our operations—

and it paid off. In less than two years, we were able to grow to thirty employees, and today, we're doing amazing.

What kept me going was the vision I saw for myself, and the grind I had to make it happen. Even though stuff would go wrong sometimes, I was determined. Throughout my life, I had learned that trials and tribulations were going to come to knock me down no matter what, but what mattered was that I kept getting back up.

Way back in CDL school, when everybody would ask each other what they wanted to do after trucking school, I told them the same vision I had then: to learn, and then take what I learned to start my own company. When Cory heard me say that and asked me to call him when I started up, I never forgot him. He had more confidence in me than some of my friends, and true to my word, I called him up. He ended up being my first employee and still works for me today!

But not everybody was as believing as he was back then. On that trip, we were all taking back from Iowa to Atlanta to find a better trucking company, my friend who was driving us didn't believe a word I was saying at the time.

But later on after everything, she told me, "Rob, when you said that to him back then, I was thinking, this dude is so cocky. How's he gonna be telling him he's gonna be working for him?"

And I can remember her looking at me in the car then like, *nigga; you don't even got two nickels to rub together!*

But she went on to tell me, "The thing I admired about

you is the fact that you had a plan and you stick to it, and you do whatever it is you say you're going to do. So when you said you were going to hire him, you did it."

While our company was taking off and starting to turn a huge profit, I ended up reconnecting with Raven again. This time around, everything was different: I was financially stable, I was in a better mental state than before, and I was ready. I wasn't going to let her get away!

In December 2019, we had our first baby girl together, and I couldn't be happier! Along with my sons, I'm glad I've been able to build something that will be a legacy from me to them. I'll be able to give my kids something that no one ever thought to give to me, and even though I was second for a long time growing up, it feels good to know that me and my family will be first for a long time.

For me, it's always been about learning from my experience and being able to make money to have freedom. And when people see my success, now and even back when I was in Alaska, they always ask me: what makes you different?

I can truly say, the only thing that makes me different from other people who had a similar situation as me in life is that I kept it in my head to strive for better. Growing up in foster care, being abused by family, feeling abandoned and struggling to survive—I knew I would have a family someday, and I would never want them to go through anything I went through.

I never stopped, never settled, and now I know my kids and fiancée won't have to either.

This is the last picture taken of my brothers and I at our sister's Latoya's funeral. That's our mom holding our youngest brother, Anthony, who I still haven't found. If you by chance know his whereabouts please email rharrisiii79@gmail.com.

ABOUT THE AUTHOR

Having served seventeen years in the military, Mr. Harris has taken his knowledge and skillset from the Army and transitioned to start a successful trucking business called Quake Logistics. Mr. Harris wants to inspire the youth and young men alike, so that they will know that where you come from doesn't determine where you will end up.

A native of Louisville, Kentucky, Mr. Harris currently resides in Atlanta, Georgia, with his fiancée Raven, sons Devron and Aaron, and daughter Robin. In his free time, he likes to watch movies (he considers Eddie Murphy as his daddy and Martin Lawrence as his uncle), cook, coach high school sports, and spend time with his family.

If you like this book, please leave a review where the book was purchased. Thanks!

 facebook.com/Robharris

 instagram.com/R.e.a.lcomedian

Made in the USA
San Bernardino, CA
20 May 2020